GW00320415

Read All About It!

Mourne Observer
Memories
from 1976-2011

Terence Bowman

Proceeds to St John's Parish Church, Newcastle, and the Donard
Fundraising Group for Marie Curie Cancer Care

© Terence Bowman 2013
All rights reserved.
No part of this book may be reproduced
without the express permission of the author
Design by Carolyn Scott
Printed by Spectator Newspapers,
Bangor, Co Down
Published by Mourne Observer Press,
Newcastle, Co Down

ISBN 978-09517833-5-1

A small number of the photographs that appear in this book (approx. 20 in total)
were published in the *Mourne Observer*. All others were taken privately at *Mourne
Observer* functions or were taken by staff photographers and were not intended for
publication in the newspaper. The author expresses his thanks to the *Mourne Observer*
for the use of copyright photographs, also to all others who supplied photographs for
this publication. The name of the photographer has been stated where it is known.

Jim Hawthorne (The Boss) with
son Will in October 1970, marking
the 21st anniversary of the Mourne
Observer's launch in 1949

This book is dedicated to the late Jim Hawthorne
(The Boss), his late son Will, the many people I
worked with at the Mourne Observer, and last, but
certainly not least, my wife Averil – who shared my
journey with them all.

Introduction

This collection of *Mourne Observer* memories had its genesis in the invitation extended towards the end of 2012 by Canon Ian Ellis, Rector of St John's Parish Church in Newcastle, to a group of journalists who live in the town. He hoped we might consider contributing a chapter each to a proposed Newcastle Journal, which would serve as a simple fundraiser for St John's.

Owing to other work commitments among the group the project had to be placed temporarily on hold; in the meantime, however, I had written a sample article recalling the first six weeks of my career at the *Mourne Observer*, which had commenced during that very memorable summer of 1976. I'd never intended to reminisce in print about my 35 years with the paper, but so encouraging was the response from Canon Ellis and a few former colleagues who had read the story, that I spent the next month delving into the furthest reaches of my memory.

The result is the book you are now holding. It would not have happened without that initial encouragement from Canon Ellis and for that reason I wish to honour the original intention, so it will be a fundraiser for St John's. A percentage of any money raised through sales of *Read all about it!* will also go to the Donard Fundraising Group for Marie Curie Cancer Care. My late mother Jean passed away at the Marie Curie Hospice (Beaconsfield) in May 1991, and the wonderfully caring staff there have the eternal gratitude of my family circle.

Please remember that many of my memories go back more than 35 years. They may differ in one way or another from how others remember the same occasion, but I have endeavoured to be as accurate as possible. The same applies to the list of those who have worked for, or been closely associated with, the *Mourne Observer* since the mid-1970s.

A small number were there before my time but deserve to be included as they worked with some of the people who are still employed at the newspaper. Should the book sell sufficiently well to merit a second print run, every effort will be made to include corrections, as well as additional names for the employee lists.

Sincere thanks go to Stephen and Alice Bleue, Nicky McKenna and Sean McConkey, as well as David and Carole Hawthorne and Mary Hawthorne, for contributing a number of the pictures that appear in the book. Also to Niki Hill for once again taking on the all-important proof-reading duties.

Terence Bowman, September 2013

The Rector writes

Surveying his many years with the *Mourne Observer*, Terence Bowman

brings that time back to life with engaging style and, where appropriate, just the right degree of humour. This is therefore a very readable book in many ways.

Of course, the years covered here saw all sorts of events – some very happy and some deeply tragic. As we look back, in whatever context, we can also learn for the future. Yet, this is not a history book – reading it is more like taking an informative journey through relatively recent times.

Proceeds from the sale of this book are being donated to St John's Church and to the Donard Fundraising Group for Marie Curie Cancer Care. This is an immensely generous gesture and I pay tribute to Terence for that generosity and for his energy and commitment to the task of writing this book.

Ian M. Ellis, September 2013

There are two Cs and two Ms in accommodation

I exercised the right of the second son to be different. My late father Hugh was a barrister and my older brother Geoffrey from an early age was determined to follow in his footsteps, preferring to practice law as a solicitor and ultimately becoming a partner with a Belfast-based legal company.

On the other hand, I was attracted to a career in journalism as I enjoyed writing and sensed a reporter's life could be very exciting with plenty of opportunities to travel the world. Little did I realise that the much-anticipated adventure would lead me all the way from my native Bangor to Newcastle – just 40 miles down the road!

Over the years I'd contributed stories to my local paper, the *County Down Spectator*. This encouraged me to apply for a place on a year-long course run by the National Council for the Training of Journalists at the College of Business Studies in Belfast. Times were very different back then; those successfully completing the course were just about promised a job.

In my case it took an interminably long three weeks (and three unsuccessful interviews, including the *Down Recorder*) before I was offered a position as a junior reporter with the *Mourne Observer*. I was 19, my first day at work was 29 June 1976, and I knew how to spell 'accommodation', which was a prerequisite for anyone joining the paper's staff.

What I'd actually been offered during an interview with Will Hawthorne four days earlier was a summer post, with no promises it would lead to anything more permanent. However, by the time I had reached Bangor he had reconsidered – swayed, he later confessed, by my enthusiasm for photography rather than any special journalistic skills I had displayed – and the full-time job was mine.

I had no wish to travel 40 miles to work each day and anyway I didn't have a car of my own, so finding somewhere to stay was high on my agenda. However, my arrival in Newcastle coincided with the beginning of the summer tourist season and in those days it was Ulster's top holiday destination, proudly lording it over the likes of Portrush and, dare I say it, Bangor.

Fortunately, a few quick phone calls by my new employer to a number of landladies around the town led me to Clara Villa, an imposing two-

storey building sitting atop the hill at the town side of King Street and overlooking South Promenade. As well as extending a warm welcome to holiday visitors, with many returning year after year, owner Merley Henderson reserved a few rooms for long-term boarders – people like me with jobs in banks, schools and local businesses that had drawn them to the town.

Clara Villa at King Street, Newcastle – a home from home for a number of new arrivals in the town

My room at the top of the stairs, with a single window overlooking King Street, wasn't quite the smallest in the house but it was a close call. And yet very quickly Clara Villa became my new home and the other boarders – like my colleagues at the *Mourne Observer* – became my new friends.

Emphasising just how long ago all this happened, Mrs Henderson charged me the princely sum of £10 each week for my room and three square meals a day. That meant a filling breakfast to start the day and a cooked dinner in the evening. I quickly discovered that walking back to King Street at lunchtime was impractical, as very often I could be sitting in a courtroom some miles away from Newcastle. Thus a greaseproof paper package containing sandwiches, an apple and a few biscuits would always be waiting for me when I set off in the morning.

Rather than being a hindrance, the lack of personal transport in the early weeks actually helped me to put down roots in Newcastle. I had access to company vehicles for the various assignments I was given, but otherwise I relied on my feet to explore the town and district. Bearing in mind it was the famous summer of '76 with wall-to-wall sunshine that lasted for two months, I had no complaints on that score.

Feeling almost like a holidaymaker, there wasn't an ice cream parlour, sweet shop or amusement arcade I didn't visit in those first few weeks of July. However, bearing in mind I was being paid just £28.60 a week by the *Mourne Observer*, such self-indulgence very quickly gave way to hikes into the nearby Mournes and extended walks along the beach, soaking up all that sunshine.

This picture, taken around September 1976, marked the departure of Hugh Hodges (third from left) and Ken Purdy (fourth from left), who were taking over the Quarter Road filling station and shop outside Annalong. Included are (from left): Hughie Carville, Evelyn Connor, Michael McClean, Nicky McKenna, Valerie Edgar (later Keown) and Clifford Mills. Ken Purdy rejoined the Mourne Observer in 1986, remaining for a further 18 months before being appointed editor of The Outlook in Rathfriland.

At the *Mourne Observer* I shared an office with Ken Purdy, the paper's senior reporter. He was just 15 when he joined the staff at the beginning of 1950 – three months after its launch. Ken immediately took me under his wing, although little did I realise he was already counting the days until his departure for a life outside journalism.

Within days Ken had introduced me to his wife Georgina (they had met in the early 1960s at the *Mourne Observer* where she worked in the darkroom – "things developed", as Ken told me), their daughter Margaret and son Andrew. Second daughter Jo was born the following July but their door was always open to me. I spent many happy evenings at the Purdy home, particularly in midweek after the paper was finished, enjoying a late supper of tea and jam sandwiches.

As far as my work as a reporter was concerned there was no sudden 'baptism of fire' after my somewhat closeted life in Bangor, where a little over a year earlier I'd still been at school. Although the Troubles had been leaving a trail of death and destruction around Northern Ireland, including South Down, there seemed to be something of a lull, at least locally, that summer.

In truth, the nearest I came to a major drama occurred when a Council meeting I was attending in Newry coincided with a riot a matter of a few hundred yards away. Rather foolishly I called my mother from a payphone outside the chamber to tell her, very excitedly, about what was happening. She hardly slept a wink that night and I quickly realised the less she knew about such matters the better it was for her peace of mind.

Will Hawthorne's second confession to me, some months later, was that he'd offered me the job without considering, or indeed caring about, any religious or political affiliations I might have. That mattered a lot to me during my working career and I still take great pride in the fact that through all my years at the *Mourne Observer* no one ever accused me of showing religious or political bias in anything I wrote or said.

It also meant that as far as reporting assignments were concerned nothing was ever off-limits. In those early days, as I worked hard to increase my shorthand speed, I was mainly entrusted with photography-based diary items that afforded me an opportunity to put together a few paragraphs as well. As a result during that July I attended the unfurling of an Orange Order banner outside Newcastle one night, followed the next by the Fleadh Cheoil in Castlewellan.

Working a minimum of five days a week, with a handy £1-an-hour overtime for night work as well, I covered hundreds of miles each week in a very battered red van, which was also used to deliver papers every Thursday morning to scores of local newsagents around a large part of the county.

There wasn't a church, school, public hall or sports ground within 20 miles of Newcastle that I didn't visit, armed with a detailed map of South Down, my notebook and trusty Pentax – the latter being my own camera from Bangor but the payback was that I could print my own photographs using the equipment in the *Mourne Observer* darkroom.

My new work colleagues fell into four categories – teenagers at the beginning of their career (some were serving a tough seven-year printer's apprenticeship and had been there for several years but were younger than me), older men and women who had been on the staff for several decades or more, part-time proof readers and members of the Hawthorne family.

The paper had been founded in October 1949 by Will's father Jim, who was still very much the figure in authority when I joined the team. Known to one and all, including his

Jim Hawthorne at his desk at 47 Main Street in October 1970, when the Mourne Observer was celebrating its 21st anniversary

own family, as 'The Boss', and famously likened by a former employee to 'an Edwardian taskmaster,' that was nowhere near the whole story. Jim Hawthorne, by then in his early 60s, led by example – there was nothing he would ask anyone to do that he wasn't prepared to do himself. Always devoted to the betterment of the *Mourne Observer*, if he could have found a way to increase the number of hours in the day or days in the week, he would have been a very happy man!

With Jim and Will at the helm, the rest of us – whether fresh-faced teenagers, middle-aged men and women with families to support or sprightly senior citizens adding a little 'pin money' to their pensions – worked together as a very tight team. When things got particularly hectic, job titles counted for nothing. That was why, for example, I found myself joining photographer John McCance early one August morning to deliver newspapers along a circuitous route that took us all the way to Comber.

Anyone who could tell one end of a camera from the other would be press-ganged into taking a picture when no one else was available. Reporters doubled up as proof readers once our stories were written and we would even take turns to answer the telephone if one of the two office girls was on leave and the other was taking her lunch break. One day, usually en route to court, we would collect adverts and the next we would deliver overdue accounts, standing patiently while the business owner scribbled out a cheque for the money he owed – or muttered an excuse about why he couldn't pay it.

Elvis Presley's death on 16 August 1977 was revealed to big fan David Hawthorne by – the author. David and his wife Carole had attended what turned out to be the legendary artist's last-ever concert, in Indianapolis on 26 June, a little under eight weeks earlier.

That's not to say there wasn't time for play as well. Within a day or two of starting I was warned to steer well clear of the lunchtime poker school in the canteen. Rumour had it that some of the veteran gamblers, who would quite happily bet on two flies climbing a window pane, could make more money during that short break than they did by doing an hour's work. I heeded the advice, at least for a time, but found it very hard to resist the 50p 'pitch and toss' challenge in the setting room, with a veritable fortune awaiting the person whose coin landed closest to the wall!

Instead of heading home at 4pm on Friday, most of the young men, along with a few of the not-so-young ones, walked or drove round to the grassy parkland at Downs Road where we divided into two teams for a kick and rush football match that usually lasted a couple of hours. In future years, out of such humble beginnings, we formed football and cricket teams, ready to take on (and very often lose to) newspaper colleagues around the Province.

It was only when I acquired my first car, a bronze-coloured 1973

Ford Escort, from John McCance for £500 in the middle of August that I began to spread my wings. I returned to Bangor most weekends to see my mother (and drop off my washing!), met up with friends in Belfast, or indeed visited places like Rostrevor, Warrenpoint and Newry that I'd first encountered when on assignments for the paper.

Had it not been for those first six weeks, when I was very quickly adopted as an unofficial son of Newcastle – to the extent that I was co-opted onto the local Town Committee (although that might have had more to do with my ability to write press releases than anything else) – I doubt very much whether the bond that continues to this day would have been so strong.

Some members of Newcastle Town Committee with Down Council assistant recreation officer Raymond Creighton (back, left) in the late 1970s. Others in back row: Archie Cairns, Bill Martin, Trevor Henderson, Aidan O'Neill. Front: Gerry Toner, Meta Stewart, Merley Henderson, Ina Cairns and Terence Bowman. Other members over the years, in addition to those who appear in the photograph, included Bill Gardiner, Fred Wadsworth, Christopher and Denize Bonny, Ronnie and Terrie Murray, Dan Smyth, Constance Higgins, Billy Newsam, Shaw Harper, Ray Deery, Jim Carphin, Anne and Hugh Davey, John and Rosaleen Torney, the Hon. Haidee Annesley, Larry McEvoy, Pat Carton, John Byrne, Bobby Thornton, Harvey Lynch, Barbara Matthews, Daphne Smart, Peta Smart, and founding chairman John Toner. In addition, there was welcome support for the Town Committee from local Councillors, including Paddy O'Donoghue, Jim Curry, Michael Boyd, Norman Bicker and Gerry Douglas.

Read All About It!

Warning to teenage reporter – do not play cards with these men (Irwyn McKibbin and Colm Murray)

Terence Bowman (left) receives the keys to his first car from previous owner John McCance. Looking on are (from second left): Clifford Mills, Sean McDowell, Michael McClean and Paul Fullam.

The Mourne Observer float promoting the 'Sweetheart of Down' beauty competition travels along the Main Street during the July 1978 summer festival parade. Those on board at that point included Clifford Mills, Sean McDowell, Sean McConkey, Eugene Bannon and Stephen Bleue.

Page Two stories

Family notices, including births, marriages and deaths, obituary reports and church announcements were always published on the second page of the *Mourne Observer*. However, as the size of the newspaper changed so too did the overall number of pages and more space would invariably be needed to accommodate all the church-related information, with their position in the paper becoming something of a moveable feast.

One thing never changed though – each story we set aside for the church notices pages was marked 'Page Two' and that remained the case long after the second page of the paper was assigned for news stories or advertising. It was a simple way of indicating that stories of a religious nature were still being treated with appropriate reverence and that was something The Boss had drummed into us from the very beginning. It was important, he stressed, that we should always respect people for whom church attendance was an important part of their lives.

From my earliest times at the *Mourne Observer* I attended a number of religious events – from the opening of a refurbished Orange Hall or a church extension to the dedication of an item of furniture donated by a grateful parishioner. However, nothing quite compared to the extended function held

A Fond Farewell for Parish Priest

Pictured from left, are; Mr. Owen Kelly, Mr. Gus McElroy, Mr. John Cavanagh (Principal of Clantygarhan Primary School), Dr. J. Maguire, Mr. Jim Flynn, Mr. Sean McArdle, Mr. Oliver Cunningham, Miss Brigid Coyle, Mr. James O'Boyle (Principal of Drumaroad Primary School), Mr. Michael Laverty and Mr. Henry O'Hare.

to mark the arrival or departure of a clergyman.

My earliest experience of this occurred at Drumaroad in March 1977, when local Parish Priest Dr Joseph Maguire (later Monsignor

Maguire) was honoured by the local community at a farewell concert prior to his departure for Downpatrick, where as Parish Priest he would serve his church faithfully for a further two decades. It became very clear to me that night how much he was loved by the people he had ministered to and how much they would miss him.

Monsignor Joseph Maguire

To my surprise, Fr Maguire set aside time to welcome me to the parish function, mentioning my presence to the audience when addressing them from the platform after receiving farewell gifts from members of the grateful congregation. It was the beginning of a long friendship which continued throughout his time in Downpatrick and into the retirement years prior to his death in 2009. Monsignor Maguire was an enthusiastic supporter of my various writing activities and would always make a point of contacting me after he'd read the latest publication.

Equally enthusiastic about my literary endeavours outside the *Mourne Observer* was the Rev. (later the Rev. Canon Dr) S. E. Long, with whom I became acquainted when he was Rector of the Grouped Parishes of Dromara and Garvaghy, a position he held between 1956 and 1985. The first time we met was

Canon S. E. Long

on a Friday night in the Spring of 1977, when the hall at St John's Church in Dromara served as the venue for an indoor bowling tournament.

I'd been despatched there by The Boss with the words "My good friend Mr Long is the rector there and I've told him to be sure to look out for you" ringing in my ears. The event, I was told, would be over by around 10.30pm but there might be a slight delay after that for the presentations. Just to be on the safe side I arrived at the hall shortly after 10pm, only to discover the competition was still in full flow. "We'll not be too much longer," I was advised by a helpful organiser.

As midnight approached, Mr Long spotted me slumped somewhat dejectedly in a corner and introduced himself. "Would you like a cup of tea, young man?" he asked. "We'll be doing the presentations shortly but we'd like to serve the refreshments first; it's been a very long night for the bowlers. We can sort out your photographs after that."

And he added: "Jim Hawthorne gave me a call earlier this evening. He told me you were a keen new recruit at his paper and wouldn't mind waiting."

What could I say when he put it so nicely? Having already worked each day and most evenings that week I would far rather have been tucked up in my bed back in Newcastle. However, I also knew if I sounded off about the delay or said I couldn't possibly wait any longer, word would have got straight back to The Boss.

So I drank my tea, waited for the presentations and then took a good selection of photographs, ensuring Mr Long was in most of them. It was well past 1am before I finally reached home. The next time I attended a function at St John's, a matter of weeks later, he greeted me like an old friend and that is the way it has been ever since.

As an interesting aside, during the mid-1990s I was conducting research for a book I

BOWLING TOURNAMENT AT DROMARA

Sponsors, prizewinners and organisers of the bowling competition appear in this picture. From left: Dr. E. Roe (of Elizabeth Alexandra Ltd.), Mrs. Mallon and Mrs. Gawley (of St. Joseph's, Lisburn), Rev. S. E. Long, Mrs. Long and Mrs. Roe.

The ladies who took part in bowling tournament at Dromara on Thursday of last week.

was writing about my great-grandfather, Alexander Bowman, a Belfast trade union pioneer and, in 1886, the first working-class Irishman to stand (unsuccessfully) for election to Westminster. I had begun the work from a standing start, not knowing anything at all about his career or his origins other than he had spent a large part of his life in Belfast.

It took several years to unravel the Alexander Bowman mystery, which to my great surprise led me to the heart of rural County Down. And the church where I learned a number of my ancestors were buried? None other than St John's in Dromara! Indeed it was Canon Long who pointed out in a lengthy review of the book that 19th Century evangelical preacher the Rev Hugh Hanna, nicknamed 'Roaring Hanna', was born in the very same Derry townland as my great grandfather.

Staying out late on a Friday night for a bowling tournament was easy enough compared to spending several hours in church on a Saturday afternoon, notebook in hand, covering the introduction of a new clergyman to his (back then it was always his) congregation. However, that was the way it was done and since it was also the era of the broadsheet newspaper – the one you couldn't read very easily on a bus – it meant typing up a near verbatim report of the entire proceedings with enough photographs to fill at least a page and sometimes more.

The *Mourne Observer* was far from alone, particularly among country newspapers, in providing such comprehensive coverage of what was, in effect, the dawning of a new era in a church's history. If the service, which could often include the ordination of the minister-to-be, was held anywhere in West Down, then the press contingent would include representatives from *The Outlook*, *Leader* and *Banbridge Chronicle*.

While such milestones in a church's life were held occasionally in the middle of the week, Saturdays were usually preferred since most people were off work and the afternoon service could be followed by a lighter celebration in the hall which could carry on well into the evening. The new clergyman would then conduct his first service the following Sunday, which very often necessitated a return visit to secure an additional picture of senior church officials.

I would contend that blame for the demise of such fulsome reporting of church events should not be laid entirely at the door of newspapers. Certainly, the decision taken by many publishers during the 1980s to adopt the new tabloid format was a contributory factor. Linked to this, the public were becoming increasingly influenced by television and radio reporting and started looking for their news in a shorter, snappier style. In truth, the new format didn't lend itself to line after line of solid type, only broken up by the occasional picture.

The churches, by adopting new technologies such as faxes and emails (and more recently social media such as Facebook and Twitter), played their own part in diminishing the traditional role of the weekly newspaper. It became very obvious to me as an editor that times were changing when invitations to send a photographer to a church event were accompanied by an advance press release, to be followed by a further 'past tense' one after it was over.

There was no longer any need to involve a reporter at all but worse than that – certainly as far as I was concerned – was the strong likelihood that without any form of embargo being imposed the story would be given a good airing in the daily papers before it could be covered in the local press.

Such enthusiasm on the part of the churches to promote their activities to as wide an audience as possible might well have ended those late nights in Dromara for a reluctant young reporter-cum-photographer, but it also reduced the previously close connection between a weekly newspaper and its local churches.

It's now some 20 years since the *Mourne Observer* last carried a very detailed report on an important event in the history of a local church – namely the arrival of the Rev. Dr (now the Rev. Canon Dr) Ian Ellis as Rector of St John's Church in Newcastle. The institution service was held on a Monday evening in August 1993 and although it was a particularly busy time at the newspaper, with a number of key people

Newcastle welcomes new rector

Dr Ian Ellis (front row, second from left), the newly instituted rector of St John's Parish Church, Newcastle, is pictured after Monday's service with (front row, from left): Mrs Letty Polson (Rector's Churchwarden), Rt Rev Dr Gordon McMullan (Bishop of Down and Dromore), Ven W B Neill (Archdeacon of Dromore), Mr Raymond Kendall (People's Churchwarden). Back row (from left): Rev T H W Dunwoody (Bishop's Chaplain), Canon Robin Greer (Rural Dean), Canon G A McCamley (Diocesan Registrar) and Ven R G Hoey (Archdeacon of Armagh).

off on holiday, I put on a shirt and tie and drove round to St John's.

I'll have to admit it wasn't entirely my own idea to take time out to report on the service. Earlier that day The Boss, still very much a commanding presence at the *Mourne Observer* despite just passing his 80th birthday, had slid open the window that separated our adjoining offices and said: "I take it we're giving the service at St John's the proper coverage the *Mourne Observer* is renowned for?" Put that way, I knew exactly where I was heading.

Silence in court!

Oone of my earliest assignments after joining the *Mourne Observer* was to attend a Friday sitting of Rathfriland Court with my reporting colleague Raymond Stewart (we were both 19 but he was my senior by almost three years, having joined the staff in September 1973).

Back in the summer of 1976, and for some years after that, virtually every local town had its own court to deal with a wide range of offences. It was an era when motorists were still being stopped by the police for offences like having a faulty tail light, a bald tyre or a defective silencer, and young people who thought it was clever to lift a bottle of milk from someone's doorstep could very quickly find themselves facing the full rigours of the law – and a criminal conviction for theft.

Sittings were held in a variety of locations, including the Royal British Legion premises at Kilkeel Harbour, the Market House in Castlewellan, the Annesley Hall in Newcastle (which was shared with the local Glee Singers), the boardroom at Warrenpoint Town Hall and even the Orange Hall in Ballynahinch.

It was also a time when the solicitors appearing in court were personalities in their own right – men like Gordon Bell in Rathfriland, Colman Hanna in

The Market House in Castlewellan today

Newcastle, Colin Flinn and Michael O'Kane in Downpatrick and Rory McShane in Newry – and very often their pleas on behalf of defendants were like private conversations with the Resident Magistrate.

The courts, which were held on one particular day or several designated days in the month, all started at 10.30am, the sole exception being the aforementioned Rathfriland sitting, which for some historical reason began at 11am. At around 10.10am on that first Friday in July Raymond stopped by my desk to tell me it was time to leave for the court as we didn't want to be late. Still new to the area and not having the least clue where Rathfriland actually was, it didn't occur to me that we were allowing ourselves a full 50 minutes to travel barely a dozen miles.

However, having reached Castlewellan in the company's trusty (rusty?) red van, Raymond instructed me to park outside a confectionery shop on the Main Street and he promptly disappeared inside. Moments later he reappeared carrying a couple of enormous ice cream cones, complete with chocolate flakes, which we proceeded to eat at a very leisurely pace.

It turned out there was a running joke among the reporters that The Boss believed the court in Rathfriland, like everywhere else, started at 10.30am and no one ever quite got round to telling him otherwise. Over the years they made a big show of getting away from the office in good time and then put their feet up for that half an hour once they were out of sight.

The Annesley Hall in Newcastle today

Unfortunately, my court days in Rathfriland were cut cruelly short, The Boss having decided over the summer that my supposed 100-words-a-minute shorthand needed sharpening – hence from the beginning of September I found myself back in a classroom, at Newcastle Tech. It meant a lot more ice cream for Raymond but I wasn't exactly complaining; I'd been enrolled for 13 weeks in a secretarial class populated entirely by teenage girls!

The court provision in Newcastle, Castlewellan and Kilkeel often left a lot to be desired – to use the modern term they were 'not fit for purpose.' Resident Magistrate Gerry Harty famously described the Annesley Hall as a "stationary iceberg" back in the 1980s, while in Kilkeel he and his colleagues would enter the court from behind a curtain, having inched their way past a large snooker table in the process.

Castlewellan Court was the only one where lawyers appearing before the RM faced the risk of physical harm. The reason for this was the ancient trapdoor in the floor of the upstairs hall in the Market House. I was present the morning a solicitor, who was new to the area, stamped his foot for dramatic effect while cross-examining a witness, only to be given a strong warning by the Clerk of Petty Sessions that it might be wiser if he stepped away from the trapdoor lest it give way under such pressure!

In Warrenpoint Town Hall all the court officials, including the Magistrate, Clerk, prosecuting and defence counsel, as well as the Press, sat around the same large table. During a particularly long and involved legal submission, I sought to relieve the boredom by ever so discreetly reading the newspaper I believed was well hidden under the table. Not so, for within a few moments a note was being passed along the length of the table until it eventually reached me. Penned by the Clerk, it warned that the Magistrate would hold me in contempt of court if I didn't immediately put away the paper.

That wasn't the only incident involving a note but on the other occasion,

Downpatrick Courthouse today

several years earlier, it didn't actually reach its intended target. At the beginning of each year Downpatrick Courthouse, that imposing building on English Street beside the Down County Museum, was the venue for the Winter Assizes – a forerunner of the Crown Court – where defendants could face very serious charges, including murder and armed robbery.

At the beginning of 1977 a very prominent person from a village in East Down pleaded not guilty to (and was subsequently acquitted of) a series of alleged thefts. The case was deemed of sufficient importance to merit verbatim coverage so Raymond and I, being the only reporters on the paper's staff at the time, other than The Boss and Will Hawthorne, travelled to the court in separate vehicles. The idea was that we would alternate, 20 minutes at a time, between taking down the evidence in shorthand and then transcribing it. At the end of the day all the pieces would then be added together into one long report.

Hearing the case was Judge James Brown, who had been a good friend of my late father's and who knew me very well from the occasional visits he still paid to our home. The court had already started when I arrived to take over reporting duties from Raymond. As I made my way to the press bench, below where the judge sat, I was the recipient of a discreet nod of recognition from His Honour.

As it happened there was a slight change of plan, with Raymond telling me I had

In 35 years of working together there was only one Raymond Stewart/ Terence Bowman lead story. Published in February 1977, it was about a plan to rebuild the much-loved Palace Cinema in Newcastle. To flesh it out there was a list of the films the intrepid pair anticipated local audiences would be flocking to see in the coming months – *The Towering Inferno, Jaws* and the little remembered *A Window To The Sky*.

to contact the office about a matter of some urgency. Thus I was in another part of the building when Judge Brown scribbled a note which was then passed to a succession of court officials before one of them tapped Raymond on the shoulder and handed it over.

"You rogue," it read, *"come and see me in my room after the court adjourns for lunch."* A bemused Raymond turned round and looked up towards Judge Brown, who quickly realised his note had reached a complete stranger!

Although they were potentially dangerous times for senior members of the legal profession, with many of their colleagues being targeted by terrorists, the magistrates who sat in the local courts very often had a sharp sense of humour. The aforementioned Gerry Harty, for example, was being addressed by a young solicitor who dared to suggest his client, who was barely in his 60s, was "an elderly man." Mr Harty gave the solicitor a withering look and uttered the immortal words: "Well he's hardly Methuselah, is he?"

Another firm favourite among the reporters was former Stormont Minister Basil McIvor who had returned to practising law after the fall of the Executive in 1974. He had little patience for plainly guilty people who wasted the court's time with frivolous denials and would often impose penalties that were intentionally excessive. He was perfectly content to see such cases going to the Appeal Court, where the phrase "that's one of Mr McIvor's cases" was uttered on a regular basis. He was equally happy to admit he didn't mind giving extra bother to people who wasted his time and that of the court.

But let's cut to the chase: on those days, usually towards the end of the week, when there was no great need to rush back to the office, where was the best after-court long lunch to be had?

There was certainly stiff competition for the accolade. Downpatrick had Dick's Cabin on Church Street. The sausage and beans there was a particular favourite and once in a while we would be joined by UTV's Gerry Kelly who was on a year's work experience with the *Down Recorder* to obtain his NUJ card. Warrenpoint had the Genoa and there was the Brass Monkey in Newry. Banbridge offered a particularly fine burger and chips at the First and Last pub on Scarva Street.

For sheer good value it was hard to beat the three-course 'Businessman's Lunch' for £1 in the Chinese restaurant along the Main

Street in Newcastle. Raymond and I usually headed there late on a Thursday afternoon after putting in a few extra hours to ensure our Downpatrick Court reports were written up for a late edition of the paper that was specifically targeted at the County Town (much to the annoyance of our rivals at the *Recorder*).

Better still was the wholesome dinner served in the Port O' Call restaurant at Bridge Street, Kilkeel. It didn't cost the weekly newspaper court reporters (usually myself, Rosemary Moreland from *The Outlook* and Jimmy Davis from the *Newry Reporter*) a single penny – the tab was always picked up by veteran Newry journalist John McAnulty who was able to claim a £3 lunch allowance from the *Belfast Telegraph*!

However, the overall winner just had to be the old-fashioned tearoom, all dainty sandwiches, Victoria sponge and chinking china cups, in Hillsborough, just opposite the village's courthouse. Back in the early 1980s I covered the monthly sitting of Hillsborough Court for our then sister paper *The Leader* in Dromore. As Friday courts went it was a breeze – and a complete waste of time – largely catering for motoring offences detected on the nearby M1. It rarely lasted more than a quarter of an hour, which meant there was always plenty of time in the tearoom across the road.

On one memorable occasion RM Basil McIvor, having arrived a few minutes early, started the court straight away – completing the final case a minute before the scheduled 10.30am starting time. A solicitor arrived red-faced and loudly complained he'd been outside consulting a client, only to be told the court books had already been signed and there was no way the sitting could be resumed.

Sad to say for all of us who regularly crammed into that tearoom, solicitors, officials and even the odd defendant, the court's days were already numbered. If memory serves me well, Hillsborough Courthouse had been protected for many years because of its close proximity to the castle and the whole royal connection. However, Northern Ireland Court Service number crunchers decided it was a big drain on valuable resources and they came up with an ingenious way to ensure they avoided any of the flak for killing off a centuries-old tradition in the village.

A new Resident Magistrate, Aidan Cullen, with a richly-deserved reputation for being an absolute stickler for every aspect of the law, was appointed and quickly made his presence felt in Hillsborough. The very first case he handled involved a defendant accused of driving without insurance. Barely 30 seconds would have been the norm at Hillsborough Court but in his hands it took more than 45 minutes. Only then was the RM completely satisfied that the punishment he imposed was appropriate to the crime. There were just six defendants on the list that day but it took nearly three hours to complete the sitting, with the same pattern being repeated over the next few months. The court officials and solicitors, who had enjoyed their easy-going Fridays in Hillsborough, realised the game was up and a campaign was launched to transfer the cases to nearby Lisburn. Needless to say, the Court Service acceded to the demand.

No one, of course, gave any thought to the tearoom and its sudden loss of valuable business!

From joy to despair

Wedding bells for Terence and Averil Bowman in August 1979. Picture by John McCance

Happily, I was not alone for the final years of the 1970s and entering the Eighties thanks to the arrival in Newcastle of my wife and life partner Averil. We had met in July 1978, just three weeks after my return to Northern Ireland following a month-long stay with a cousin in Canada, during which I'd made semi-serious enquiries about the possibility of emigrating and finding work over there. By that stage I'd completed two years with the *Mourne Observer*, which was generally accepted within the industry as adequate for anyone planning a move into the daily papers, radio or even television.

Averil was also from Bangor, prompting Will Hawthorne to quip that the 'lasses' in Newcastle had learned to give me a wide berth, being well aware of the long hours I was working and their impact upon anything approaching a social life. We became engaged in early December that same year and Averil was formally introduced to my *Mourne Observer* colleagues at the annual Christmas party in the town's Harbour Inn.

My abiding memory of that night is of being escorted to the bar – some might say dragged – by John McCance and Irwyn McKibbin to treat everyone to a round of drinks. Thankfully the hour was late and the bill for our entire group amounted to a little under £5.

Averil and I were married by the Rev. (later Canon) Noel Warren at St John's Church in Newcastle on 25 August 1979. John did the honours as official wedding photographer and his able colleague Eugene Bannon was on hand with an 8mm cine camera. Averil discovered very quickly that Will's quip wasn't so far off the mark – as someone considerably more famous than any of us once remarked: "Well, there were three of us in this marriage." In our case it was the *Mourne Observer* and wedded bliss ultimately had little impact on my busy work schedule.

Most weeks I would set off for the office, admittedly a short three-minute drive from our home, at 9am on Monday and, apart from meal breaks, the first time Averil would attract anything approaching my attention was on Wednesday, after the paper was printed. Not unsurprisingly, and given her previous experience as a pharmacy manager in Bangor, she accepted a job offer from a local chemist within a fortnight of our return from honeymoon.

All the same, they were good years for us and they were good years for the *Mourne Observer*, which had been enjoying regular circulation increases ever since its launch back in 1949. Staff-wise, the three years following my arrival had witnessed the appointment of a number of new members who would

Celebrating their close-fought victory over Newcastle Round Table in a Combat Cancer pub quiz, held at the Brook Cottage Hotel in May 1978, are 'The Roadsweepers', comprising (from left): Cllr Eamonn O'Neill, Raymond Creighton, Terence Bowman, David Parkhill and Bryan Coburn

go on to give the paper many years of dedicated service, among them Sean McConkey, Eugene Bannon, Stephen Bleue, Irene McGrady, Isabell Hamilton, Raphael Mason and Alice Kerr (who, upon her marriage to Stephen in 1983, became Alice Bleue).

Having moved from 47 Main Street to a newly-constructed office complex on the Castlewellan Road back in 1975, the next stage in the paper's expansion saw the construction of an extension to house a larger printing press as the decade drew to a close.

Will Hawthorne oversaw the latter work, which involved dismantling and transporting four heavy units from several different presses he had purchased in Scotland and the Republic, including Ennis, County Clare (from *The Clare Champion* newspaper, which had just changed over to web-offset printing), and then reassembling them into one single printing press back in Newcastle.

Dismantling the former Clare Champion printing press at Ennis, County Clare, in 1979 are (from left): Will Hawthorne, Nicky McKenna, Colm Murray, Sean McConkey and John McCance

It was, without doubt, his crowning glory as a newspaper man and he was assisted in the work by a crew from the paper, including, variously, Colm Murray, Sean McConkey, John McCance, Nicky McKenna, Stephen Bleue and Michael McClean.

Once the new printing press was operating at full capacity in the early 1980s we could produce a 32-page broadsheet *Mourne Observer* each week, compared to a previous maximum of 24 pages and even that had involved two separate print runs. Our other printing press, which was

Heavy lifting gear is needed to complete the task

located within the main factory area, was retained for our sister paper *The Leader*. Weekly sales of the *Mourne Observer* reached almost 15,000 copies – then, as now, the largest of any newspaper circulating within County Down – while *The Leader* notched up a very impressive tally of 6,500 sales.

In the early summer of 1981 Raymond and I also welcomed Diane Forbes, a new colleague in the editorial department. She was our very first female reporter and, like myself, was a product of the journalism course at the College of Business Studies in Belfast. Her classmates included Paul Symington and Gary Law, who both subsequently joined the *Down Recorder*.

Hughie Carville (centre) serves the tea to production staff members around 1980. From left: Stephen Bleue, Kenny Cromie, Nicky McKenna, Sean McDowell, Sean McConkey, Eugene Bannon, Michael McClean and Raphael Mason.

Not long afterwards, Will sent the two of us to Banbridge to conduct vox pop street interviews for a survey aimed at determining if there were aspects of the paper that needed strengthening. We tried our best but it proved difficult to find people so far from our Newcastle base who actually read the *Mourne Observer* and even if they did to then provide a forensic analysis of its contents. In

Mourne Observer Memories

Music was my first love
And it will be my last
Music of the future
And music of the past

To live without my music
Would be impossible to do
In this world of troubles
My music pulls me through

For Stephen Bleue (words and music by John Miles)

the end Diane and I beat a hasty retreat to a local cafe and filled in a pile of survey sheets by pretending we were readers of varying ages and backgrounds ("Okay, you be a widow who lives on a farm and

Sam Maxwell (back) and Irwyn McKibbin work by candlelight during a power cut in the early 1980s

Harry Polland was the Mourne Observer's senior typesetter for a number of years. Having served his apprenticeship with the paper in its early years, he moved to the Irish News but returned to his home area paper in 1966. Harry passed away in July 1983 and is fondly remembered by the family circle, Mourne Observer colleagues and by his many friends in the Newcastle Comhaltas branch, where he served as chairman for 13 years.

reads the paper from cover to cover, I'll be a middle-aged worker from the shoe factory who enjoys the sport"). We handed Will the completed sheets and were commended for our sterling efforts!

That wasn't my first involvement with a readership survey. Back in 1977 we had conducted a similar venture, only that time the paper printed a form so readers could submit their views on the various columns we published, our news and sports coverage, and whatever else they wanted to see in the paper. Better still, there were cash prizes for the best entries. At that point in my career I hadn't the nerve to tell The Boss and Will how I would improve the *Mourne Observer* so, instead, I filled in the form using a bogus name.

'James Taylor' from the Castlewellan Road in Newcastle didn't have much time for Broadmeadow's farming page or Gay Spark's fashions but was a big fan of the rather excellent pop column by that new reporter the

Mourne Observer had just recruited.

While they disagreed with my observations about farming and

fashions, they nevertheless decided my comments merited a cash prize of £3. I didn't dare own up to being 'James Taylor', which meant that, despite The Boss's dogged but ultimately unsuccessful efforts to track him down, the money went to charity.

As with its gleaming new printing press, the *Mourne Observer* was running like a well-oiled machine as we reached the mid-Eighties. Although we were all still working ridiculously long hours, the team spirit had never been stronger, with the annual Christmas party always the highlight of our year. My own career at the paper, which back in 1978 had appeared to be drawing to a close, continued apace with added responsibilities, moving into a fifth, sixth and then a seventh year.

And then, on Saturday 11 February 1984, the sudden and unbelievable death of Will Hawthorne, after he suffered a massive heart attack in Belfast while playing rugby for

his beloved Ballynahinch Evergreens, brought the world he had played such an important part in creating, crashing down around us. He was just 43.

Losing Will was devastating for his wife Mary, sons Paul and Michael and daughter Heather, parents Jim and Charlotte, his sisters Lottie, Mary, Maureen and Evelyn, his brother David and the wider family circle. For the shocked staff, who mourned the passing of a friend and mentor, it would be no exaggeration to say that, in one way or another, our lives were irrevocably changed by Will's death. Even the passage of so many years has not changed that view.

The very next afternoon the senior staff were brought together by Clifford Mills, our production manager and the company's longest serving employee, at The Boss's home on the Shimna Road. We were there not only to express, individually and collectively, our heartfelt sympathy to the grieving Hawthorne family, but also to reassure them that, as Will would have wanted, work would continue on that week's edition of the *Mourne Observer*.

Will's funeral service was held at Newcastle Presbyterian Church the following Tuesday afternoon, by which time a host of touching tributes had been paid by representatives from every sphere of public and sporting life, along with others penned by friends and colleagues from not only the *Mourne Observer* but also a large number of newspapers from across the Province.

Responsibility for putting together Will's obituary report was entrusted to me, and although I was greatly assisted by David and his father in my endeavours, no words of mine – at the age of 26 – seemed adequate when it came to articulating how influential a presence Will had been in all our lives.

In the end, and perfectly understandably, publication of that week's paper was delayed by some hours because of the funeral and its aftermath. The important thing, however, was that we did get the *Mourne Observer* into the shops – we were still very much in business.

The Rt. Rev. Dr. Howard Cromie, Moderator of the General Assembly of the Presbyterian Church, and Mrs Cromie paid a visit to the Mourne Observer on 5 November 1984. They are pictured with (from left): Jim Hawthorne, David Hawthorne, Terence Bowman and the Rev. Andrew McComb, Senior Minister of First Dromara Presbyterian Church, who was accompanying the Moderator.

Over the following months there was much readjusting, in various ways, for everyone associated with the paper. However, with The Boss the backbone of the *Mourne Observer* and David, supported by his wife Carole, taking on ever greater responsibilities, we somehow managed to maintain the steady progress of earlier years.

I took over responsibility for a set of features on Ballynahinch, as seen through the eyes of local man George Burrowes, which Will had been planning prior to his death. What had initially been intended as a short summer series ended up running in the paper for six months. For my efforts I was privileged to receive a Rothmans Press Award for 1985.

All the same, as the years passed by there was a general acceptance that, certainly in production terms, the *Mourne Observer* was beginning to fall well behind a number of our

Tom Rainey (left), operations manager with Rothmans N. Ireland, presents the £100 prize to Terence Bowman of the Mourne Observer in October 1985

rivals. Once again The Boss was to the forefront in encouraging the major production changes we began to introduce. It was far from plain sailing because we wanted to blend the old and new, thereby allowing us to continue printing the paper in Newcastle.

For a couple of years we put together a *Mourne Observer* that, not entirely successfully, married our long-established hot metal system with a 'paste-up' process derived from computer typesetting, along with pictures engraved onto photopolymer plates. Our task was made all the harder after the *Down Recorder* brought forward deliveries to early on a Wednesday morning. Rather than risk losing vital early sales we had to match them and that meant working non-stop on Tuesday night until the paper was finished. Most of the senior staff would arrive for work in daylight and head home in daylight, the night having come and gone in the meantime.

Eventually we had to concede that serious changes would be necessary if we wanted to maintain our position as the area's top-selling weekly newspaper and a contract was signed with Morton Newspapers to have the *Mourne Observer* printed at their works in Portadown. Following the installation of computers in all departments – including Amstrad word processors that used floppy disks containing about one megabyte of memory for the reporters – and a number of dry runs, we were ready for the transformation, which also involved reducing the paper in size from broadsheet to European tabloid.

The most immediate impact on the staff was a new and considerably earlier Tuesday deadline of around 7.30-8pm. It also meant an end to those two consecutive and very punishing late working nights.

The first new-look *Mourne Observer* went to press late on 25 April 1989, although following a number of unscheduled stops and starts the print run wasn't completed until early the following morning. David and I had travelled over to Portadown to witness that little bit of history and to help organise deliveries which were being undertaken by our own staff. Shortly after 4am we arrived back at The Boss's house with the very first copies to reach Newcastle. He was still up, pacing around the kitchen.

Handing him a copy of the paper, dated Wednesday 26 April, we awaited his verdict. He turned each page very slowly and very deliberately, checking the headings didn't contain any howlers and that the ink levels had been given the same care that had been his trademark over the years.

David and Jim Hawthorne in a picture taken to mark the 40th anniversary of the Mourne Observer in October 1989

His response was very positive and very simple: "We should have done it years ago."

That same October we published an eight-page supplement, including photographs of the management along with staff members at work and past reporters' recollections, to mark the paper's first 40 years. In addition there were two dinners, one at the Slieve Donard Hotel for the current staff and the other at the Brook Cottage Hotel for former and retired employees, mainly reporters, who had been there during the formative years. We had every reason to celebrate the paper's ruby anniversary, but we also paused to remember our absent friends.

Will Hawthorne, a keen supporter of the Newcastle branch of the Royal National Lifeboat Institution, was presented with the Silver Lifeboatman Award in acknowledgment of his efforts on behalf of the organisation. Here he can be seen (right) on board the town's new lifeboat, The Jane Hay, as it arrives at the local harbour after its maiden voyage in 1980.

Sally Bingham operates the keyboard of one of the new teletypesetting machines, which were first introduced in the early 1980s. The resulting punched tape was fed into a Heath Robinson-esque contraption attached to a specially converted linotype machine (the workings of which, it seemed, were known only to Sean McConkey), thereby producing lines of lead type.

Production night at the Mourne Observer in the mid-1980s. With Hughie Carville in the foreground, the others include Sean McConkey, Sam Maxwell, Jim Hawthorne, Colm Murray and David Hawthorne.

Typical of the Ballynahinch Evergreens, when Will Hawthorne (right) was awarded the Murray Cup as Evergreens Player of the Year (for 1982-83) in October 1983, he and Martin Murray, presenter of the cup, hiked to the top of Slieve Donard to make the accompanying photograph look a little more interesting!

Read All About It!

Colleagues marked the retirement of part-time typesetter Anthony Heaney (second from left) in November 1988. He had served his apprenticeship with the Mourne Observer back in 1954 before emigrating to Australia. He spent the final 14 years of his working life back at the paper. From left: Sean McDowell, Colm Murray, Clifford Mills and Nicky Cunningham.

Education Minister Brian Mawhinney visited the Mourne Observer during its 40th anniversary year (1989). Included are Jim Hawthorne, David Hawthorne, Terence Bowman and (at front) the two Seans, McConkey and McDowell.

Current and former staff members from the 1950s, 1960s and early 1970s attended a dinner to mark the 40th anniversary of the Mourne Observer in October 1989. Back (from left): Terence Bowman, Terry McLaughlin, Martin Waddell, Michael Drake, Dominic Cunningham, Brad Fleming, David Hawthorne. Front: Stanley Maxwell, Jim Hawthorne and Ken Purdy.

'It was the best of times, it was the worst of times...'

THAT quotation from *A Tale of Two Cities*, penned by Charles Dickens more than 150 years ago, perhaps sums up better than any the life of most – if not all – journalists who faced the challenge of living and working in Northern Ireland during the final three decades of the 20th Century.

While I would never seek to compare the work we did with our pens, notebooks and cameras to the pain and suffering experienced by countless thousands during the Troubles, all the same many in our profession, and that includes 'ordinary' weekly newspaper reporters and photographers like myself and my colleagues, witnessed sights that will stay with us for the rest of our lives.

Very early one Sunday morning in August 1977, for example, I was barely 20 and still very much a junior reporter when I dashed from my King Street 'digs' to the back of the Slieve Donard Hotel just minutes after a large bomb was detonated underneath a 1,600-gallon propane gas tank.

It created a fierce atomic bomb-like fireball, with burning gas being blasted in all directions. Seven people standing nearby sustained horrific injuries and two cars – one of them occupied – were badly damaged. A warning had been given but – mercifully – the bomb went off before the hotel was evacuated. Had the hundreds of dancers been milling around the gas tank when the explosion occurred, the death toll would have been unimaginable.

In complete contrast, a couple of days later I found myself rubbing shoulders with The Queen and Prince Philip during their Silver Jubilee

visit to Hillsborough Castle. That's no exaggeration for, despite some of the tightest security ever witnessed in Northern Ireland, the atmosphere within the castle grounds was surprisingly relaxed.

When the garden party attended by many local people was over and it was time for the royal couple to leave, they were a matter of feet from me as they walked through a gate en route to their helicopter which was sitting in a secluded part of the castle grounds.

Those two stories appeared side by side on the front page of that week's *Mourne Observer*, along with comprehensive coverage of the busy holiday season in Newcastle and the Mournes, indicating in very stark terms the role the newspaper played in reporting the best and worst aspects of life in our community.

In truth, for every story about families enjoying themselves during the holiday season in

Smiles all round during the garden party hosted by The Queen at Hillsborough Castle in August 1977

Newcastle, there was a painfully detailed report on a murder, a funeral or a town centre devastated by a car bomb. During one short period in the mid-1980s David Hawthorne and I attended Troubles-related funerals on three successive Sundays.

I must have covered hundreds of Council meetings during my first couple of decades with the newspaper. For the most part they were long and usually dull affairs, producing a veritable mountain of stories that filled many pages but I imagine went largely unread. Only the tea break with the promise of a couple of biscuits (Down District Council) or a plate of sandwiches and cream buns (Newry and Mourne) offered any relief from the boredom.

In the aftermath of an atrocity, however, the change in the atmosphere was palpable. Angry accusations flew in all directions, with some Councillors holding others, because of their politics or even their religion, directly or indirectly responsible for bombings and murders or at any rate being supportive of the perpetrators' actions.

They were very tense times and certainly as far as the Councils I attended were concerned, such bitterness and rancour continued, with barely a break, from my earliest days through to the 1994 ceasefires and even beyond.

That's not to say Council meetings were entirely cheerless gatherings. Seamus Byrne, Down District Council's long-serving Clerk and Chief Executive, operated a well-reasoned policy when matters of a sensitive nature, including issues relating to individual members of staff, were being discussed. While other local authorities ordered reporters out of the chamber when they went 'into committee', Seamus reckoned that by allowing us to stay put we would be party to delicate discussions and would therefore feel obliged to respect their confidentiality.

So night after night we would sit in the chamber with our pens down waiting for the public part of the meeting to resume. Such delays could be quite tedious which was why on one particular occasion I sidled up to my two *Down Recorder* colleagues who were occupying their customary seats in a raised area beside the door. As far as any curious Councillors were concerned we were engaged in a quiet conversation, whereas in fact we were busily playing poker, complete with small piles of coins that moved around as the games progressed. There was a sigh of genuine disappointment from at least one of us when the Clerk brought the private discussions to a close!

Over at Newry and Mourne Council successive chairmen operated a very welcome policy whereby at the end of often long and fractious sessions the 'cabinet' was opened to all those who had managed to stick

Read All About It!

An apology was sought back in December 1983 after the above headline appeared over a picture taken in Kilkeel, which included leading DUP members Ian Paisley and Peter Robinson, along with their wives and future South Down DUP Assembly member Jim Wells. A DUP spokesman told the Mourne Observer somewhat tersely: "We don't dance at our dinners."

it out to the end, including Councillors, officials and the Press. Political enemies, who had spent much of the meeting hurling insults at each other, would call a temporary truce to hostilities to enjoy a drink together, funded from the chairman's annual allowance.

This was long before the tobacco ban was introduced so anyone joining the late night soiree also had to contend with clouds of smoke from cigarettes, cigars and even a few pipes. A *Mourne Observer* colleague once left the Council offices at 5am on a Tuesday, having arrived for the meeting some 10 hours earlier. Amazingly, by 9am he was back at his desk clattering away on his typewriter!

Incidentally, I have a small personal claim to fame with regard to a particularly divisive period at Newry and Mourne District Council back in 1990. It all stemmed from the introduction of a controversial committee structure by the SDLP majority, a decision viewed by many as being their revenge for the three years Newry Independent

Councillor Eugene Markey had served as chairman, backed by a so-called 'unholy alliance' of Unionist, Independent and Republican representatives.

No work of any significance was completed by the local authority – indeed, no fewer than 24 special Council meetings were called to challenge decisions taken at committee level. The exchanges between members became increasingly bitter, occasionally involving threats of physical violence. The whole nasty business went on for five months.

I wrote a front page editorial (below, left) which was, in effect, a personal plea to Councillors to sort out their differences and get back to work for the sake of an already fractured community. The tactic apparently worked as normal business did indeed resume the following week – and continued, dare I say it, until they found something else to row about.

But at least they were still serving sandwiches and cream buns at the tea break and the chairman was still opening his cabinet after the meetings!

Two good men among many

In advance of delivering a talk to a local history group a while back, I set about trying to determine precisely how many Troubles-related deaths had been covered by the *Mourne Observer* during my years as a reporter and later as Editor.

Since the total would of necessity include military personnel, as well as police officers and civilians, I guessed it would be quite high, bearing in mind that at one time or another the paper's circulation area took in all of Down District, a substantial part of Newry and Mourne and an equally large part of Banbridge District, including Rathfriland and Banbridge itself (which explains why we produced three different editions back in the early 1980s).

Although I had reported on many of the deaths myself, either by covering the incidents that had led to a loss of life or the resulting funerals, nothing quite prepared me for the answer. I calculated that some 60 deaths between 1976 and 1980 could be attributed to the conflict, while the overall total, up to and including 1994, easily topped the 200 mark.

The Troubles claimed the lives of many people from Newcastle and district but I knew very few of them on anything approaching a personal level. My own roots were in Bangor and North Down; had I been born and raised in South Down, I have little doubt I would have lost friends and quite possibly relatives to terrorist violence.

While reluctant to single out individual incidents or victims, to spare the families further heartbreak, I would, nevertheless, like to mention two good men I met and got to know very well during the course of my work.

In early January 1987 I attended a cheque presentation ceremony at the Brook Cottage on the Bryansford Road. I'd taken the call myself and agreed to go along, camera in hand, after being told there were security concerns because of the involvement of senior police personnel.

It transpired that sizeable sums were being presented to two good causes, the Newcastle Drop-In Centre and the St John Ambulance Cadets, by Inspector David Ead and Superintendent Alwyn Harris, the latter being the RUC Sub-Divisional Commander and therefore in overall charge of policing in the area. I already knew both men – we were on 'nodding' terms – because they attended local courts to prosecute police cases and my duties still included court reporting.

After the pictures were taken there was time to relax and the two men were genuinely interested in hearing more about the *Mourne Observer* representative they had seen in court, notebook in hand, but who was now carrying a camera. I learned that evening how David Ead was a former soldier who originally came from Plymouth, while Alwyn Harris had been in the RUC long enough to remember my father representing clients in the same courts he had attended as a young officer.

Our paths crossed from time to time over the next few months, with those nods being replaced by friendly waves. Then, on 20 April 1987 – Easter Monday – David Ead was shot dead by the IRA while he patrolled on foot near the Central Promenade entrance to Donard Park. I was in the town that night and was struck by the grim reality of life, and death, in Northern Ireland, namely that while that end of the town was sealed off by the security forces as they carried out their investigations into the murder, elsewhere in the seaside town it was very much business as usual.

I sent a personal letter of condolence to Supt. Harris. He responded with an equally personal response, indicating he had forwarded my note to the Ead family with the hope they would draw some strength and comfort from it and many others "in the lonely weeks, months and years ahead." I was later approached by a member of David's family in Plymouth who said his relatives very much preferred my relaxed picture of him, taken at the Brook Cottage, to the more formal one issued by the RUC, and it subsequently appeared in his local papers as well as the *Mourne Observer*.

Two-and-a-half years later, on 8 October 1989, Alwyn Harris was killed when an IRA bomb exploded under his car as he drove to church in Lisburn to attend a Harvest Thanksgiving service. He was on extended sick leave at the time due to a serious heart condition. His wife was also in the car but, mercifully, she escaped with minor injuries.

A second letter, again voicing my sympathy at the loss of a dedicated officer I'd come to know, was acknowledged by the Deputy Sub-Divisional Commander, Chief Inspector Tom Ferguson.

David and Alwyn were two good men among many from all sections of the community who lost their lives in the Troubles – none of them will ever be forgotten.

Climb every mountain

Having the Mourne Mountains right on our own doorstep was very handy for those among us – certainly in our younger days – who were attracted by the prospect of some really strenuous exercise.

My first serious encounter with the upper reaches of the mountains occurred at Christmas 1976, some six months after I joined the *Mourne Observer*. Over the preceding months, despite my own best efforts, I'd never managed to get past the icehouse, just beyond the tree line, having been let down by a succession of friends from Bangor who announced they wanted to climb Slieve Donard but very quickly ran out of steam.

With the office closed and no new paper until New Year I was back in my home town for a break. I was already beginning to wonder if the whole *Mourne Observer* experience had been a long and very vivid dream when Will rang to see if I'd like to join him and his young son Paul for a hike into the mountains.

Having done little else but eat and watch television over the holidays, I readily agreed and we met at Donard Park early the following morning, 29 December. I surprised even myself by managing to keep up with the pair of them as we made our way through the forest, passed the icehouse and within an hour or so had made it to The Saddle, where we paused for a hot drink. Our plan was to mount an assault from there on the summit of Slieve Donard but it very quickly came unstuck – thanks to a very elementary mistake on my part.

While I'd ensured I was wearing plenty of warm clothing with spares of everything in a backpack, as instructed by Will, I let myself down in the footwear department. Instead of wearing proper climbing boots for the mid-winter outing, I'd opted for the comfort of the same shoes I normally wore to work. They had rubber soles and I was unable get any sort of grip in the rock-hard snow we encountered during the final stages of the ascent.

We had no other option but to abandon our target, much to my disappointment, and to take an alternate homeward route after climbing over the Mourne Wall. Even then we were greeted by sheets of thick ice in many places, which really put my shoes to the test. Paul, who was eight at the time, began to feel the strain in his young legs and his dad carried him for trickier parts of the descent. We eventually made it to the Trassey Road where, by good fortune, we were able to thumb a lift most of the way back to Newcastle. Piping hot vegetable soup, courtesy of Will's wife Mary, made it a perfect end to a decidedly challenging day.

Eight-year-old Paul Hawthorne shows Terence Bowman the correct way to dress when attempting to climb Slieve Donard in the middle of the winter (late December 1976). Picture by Will Hawthorne

More than a year passed before the subject of the Mournes was raised again, by which time I had acquired a pair of sensible boots that had seen little or no action. Will was planning to take part in the annual Mourne Wall Walk, scheduled for early June 1978, and came up with the idea of putting together a team from the paper to tackle the gruelling 22-mile route, which took in most of the main peaks, including Slieve Donard.

A small number of us, including Sean McConkey, Stephen Bleue, Michael McClean, John McCance and myself, stepped forward – or was it more the case that everyone else stepped backwards? Either way, for most Sundays during May we undertook regular practice sessions that became longer and longer and took us higher and higher into the mountains. We never completed the entire route in one go but those dry runs were certainly enough to give us an idea of exactly what lay ahead on 4 June.

Team numbers gradually dwindled for one reason or another – Sean McConkey, for example, hurt his foot one Sunday and had to be accompanied back to the car park to receive treatment, while I realised there was too much risk of sustaining a serious injury just a few days before my planned month-long holiday in Canada. All the same, I did finally conquer Slieve Donard with John McCance a week before the Mourne Wall Walk.

John, Michael and Will all completed the Walk in very commendable times and I made sure I was there to take the pictures that proved it. I travelled by car and then on foot to reach the most easily-accessible point on Slieve Binnian that I knew the large army of walkers would pass. It was then just a matter of waiting for the *Mourne Observer* trio to reach my vantage point. Had the expression "I can feel your pain" been in common usage at that time, I'm pretty sure I would have used it.

A further decade would elapse, with numerous staff members coming and going in the meantime, before there would be one final Mournes outing. The paper had been most fortunate in 1987 to engage the part-time services of James (Jim) Aiken, who had just retired from the *Belfast Telegraph*'s production team. Highly skilled and with a lifetime of experience in the industry, he was recruited by The Boss and David to

Will Hawthorne takes a breather during his successful completion of the Mourne Wall Walk in June 1978

Michael McClean takes it all in his stride

John McCance was hoping for a snappy finish

help steer our staff through the challenging transitional stage between the old and new technologies. He enjoyed it so much that in the end he stayed with the paper for 12 years.

Away from his work, Jim was an enthusiastic walker and mountain climber who during many summer holidays had tackled most of Europe's higher peaks. Hence, in early May 1988, hoping to spread the

The intrepid team of Mourne hikers in May 1988 (from left): Valerie Keown with daughter Julie, Evelyn Connor, Kathleen Braniff, Edna Prytherch, Averil Bowman, Terence Bowman, Jim Aiken, Stephen Bleue, Sean McDowell and Michael McKenna. Picture by Nicky McKenna.

message, he invited *Mourne Observer* colleagues, men and women alike, to join him for a Saturday morning hike in the Mournes. Those accepting included two survivors from the 1978 Mourne Wall Walk 'rehearsals', Stephen Bleue and myself, along with Nicky McKenna, Sean McDowell, Valerie Keown, May Magee, Kathleen Braniff, Evelyn Connor and Edna Prytherch, plus my wife Averil, Valerie's daughter Julie and Nicky's son Michael, with, of course, Jim as group leader.

We parked the cars on the Slievenaman Road, a short distance from Spelga Dam, and set our sights on reaching the Blue Lough, located in a col between Silent Valley and the Annalong Valley.

Taking a rest after climbing Doan in May 1988 (from left): Sean McDowell, Stephen Bleue, Terence Bowman, Michael McKenna, Averil Bowman and Nicky McKenna.

We'd all followed Jim's advice and were wearing stout walking boots – with one very obvious exception. Kathleen Braniff, from Annacloy, completed the entire walk to the Blue Lough and back wearing a pair of bright green stiletto-heeled shoes. Her seemingly incongruous footwear had raised concerns when we first met up at the *Mourne Observer* car park. However, Kathleen reasoned that they offered her the greatest comfort and the fact she finished the day without so much as a blister suggested she might have had a point.

Wisely, Kathleen had opted not to join a party comprising Jim, Stephen, Sean, Nicky and Michael, Averil and myself who tackled nearby Doan – deemed by the guide books as a modest climb but nevertheless involving an ascent of some 1,300ft. Standing on the summit, surveying the majestic Mournes all around us, was without doubt the highlight of the day.

Looking back with the benefit of hindsight, nothing was ever more representative of the wonderful team spirit that existed at the *Mourne Observer* back in the 1980s than Jim Aiken's never-to-be repeated mountain adventure.

Stephen Bleue (left) and Terence Bowman
survey the majestic Mournes

Headline news

O n the mercifully few occasions (certainly from the audience's point of view) when I have been invited to give a talk about my career at the *Mourne Observer*, the question will inevitably arise about which stories linger the longest in my memory.

They fall generally into two categories – those I wrote myself, for the most part during my earlier days as a roving reporter, and the remainder, comprising the majority, which were contributed by members of our reporting team, either upon my instruction or through their own initiatives.

Members of the Newcastle Business and Professional Women's Club with guest speaker Terence Bowman, accompanied by his wife Averil, at their Christmas dinner in December 1987. Also included (from left): Eileen Fullerton (treasurer), Shirley Hodgkins, Dorothea Nicholson (president), Dorothy Jackson and Ruth Graffin.

I have a soft spot for a number of the stories I penned during my first few months in Newcastle, when so much was still new to me. Very often I shared the very obvious excitement of the person I was interviewing and hopefully reflected that in my report of their particular achievement.

Back in the 1970s, the *Mourne Observer* had a network of local contributors – people like Nicky McConville in Kilkeel, David Biggerstaff in Ballyward, Raymond Barry in Downpatrick, Woodrow Graham in Ballynahinch, Harry McCandless in Dromore and Paul McEvoy in Warrenpoint (now a nonagenarian and still submitting work to the paper) – who would regularly tip off the paper about happenings in their community. In that decidedly pre-mobile phone era, to cover any story properly involved driving to the scene, co-ordinating with the news source and then, ideally, interviewing the person involved.

Some of my reports would now seem somewhat bizarre when judged against the modern definition of what constitutes a good story; little wonder they are the ones that stick most in the mind. A particular favourite from 1976 involved the discovery by an awestruck child of a weather balloon that had broken free from its tether and then crashed to earth in a farmer's field miles from anywhere. As far as that

Mourne Observer Memories

Raymond Stewart, a dab hand at playing the cornet, appeared on the front cover of *Record Mirror* on 14 January 1978. Actually this isn't true. Someone who looked like Raymond Stewart appeared on that front cover.

child, raised on a diet of *Doctor Who* and *Star Trek*, was concerned, it just had to be an alien spaceship; all that was missing was the pointy-eared occupants.

Standing beside the 'alien spaceship' which had spilled its electronic wizardry onto the ground, the excited child blurted out his story and then stood, proud as Punch, for a photograph. Within days, I'm sure, he was reading through every line of the story I'd written for that week's paper, dismissing out of hand the Met Office's explanation that it was just a weather balloon.

In the summer of 1980 I wrote a series of stories that prompted a visit to Newcastle by a team from the BBC's *Checkpoint* radio programme, led by renowned investigative journalist Roger Cook. Reports had started circulating locally about the seemingly amazing results that were being achieved with cancer sufferers at a clinic operating on the outskirts of the town. While none of those working at the clinic, which specialised in a form of cranial osteopathy, dared

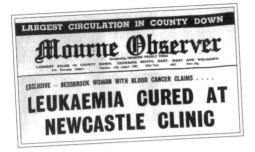

to suggest they were actually curing cancer, nevertheless they encouraged a number of their patients, previously diagnosed with leukaemia, to speak out. All insisted they were making a remarkable recovery and were resuming a normal life.

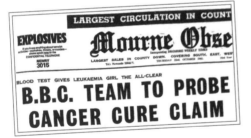

News of the claims spread to the daily and national press and before the end of the year Roger Cook had checked in at the Slieve Donard Hotel. He conducted a series of probing interviews with the same people I had spoken to and there was little doubt they genuinely believed the clinic had offered them a new lease of life.

The toughest questioning was reserved for the head of the clinic, with Roger Cook placing considerable emphasis on the notion of remission – that the patients had been given a little extra time, but no more than that, and any suggestion they were getting their lives back was deceiving them in the worst possible way.

The programme was broadcast on the Radio Four network in the run-up to Christmas and to my mind ended in a draw. Both sides scored points but there was no overall winner and in time the clinic dropped out of the headlines.

There's an interesting tailpiece to the story. Around five years later I was having lunch with my late father's best friend who was the local doctor in a village some 25 miles from Newcastle. A woman I had interviewed for the clinic story in 1980 just happened to be one of his patients and I enquired how she was doing. Half expecting to be told she had passed away a few years earlier, I was pleasantly surprised to learn she was still alive and indeed leading a perfectly normal life. As for her doctor, who confirmed there had been an earlier terminal diagnosis, he could offer no rational explanation, other than an extended remission period, for her continuing good health.

"We have been in touch with our allies this morning. We have discussed what the Iraqis have had to say and I have spoken to President Bush. We have co-ordinated our response to what they have had to say and on behalf of the allies the President will make that public at some stage later this afternoon..."

Those words by Prime Minister John Major, which all but signalled the launch of the first Gulf War's land offensive, were carried in the *Mourne Observer* under the front page banner headline 'History in the making' on 27 February 1991.

Prime Minister John Major with managing directors Gerry and Florence Barlow during his visit to the Typerite factory in Warrenpoint

There was a simple reason why a weekly newspaper in Northern Ireland was dipping a toe into the world of international politics. Mr Major was paying a courtesy visit

to the Typerite factory in Warrenpoint and two of our reporters, David Telford and Amy Dempster, were there, rubbing shoulders with press representatives from around the globe, when the Prime Minister suddenly interrupted the tour to converse with President Bush. The rest, as they say, was indeed history and by all accounts the office telephone used by Mr Major was later disconnected and put on display at the factory.

A 'Kronik' effort!

With the obvious exception of our own Troubles, few events captured as much front page attention, in a very short space of time, as the 1991 Gulf War. In addition to those Major/ Bush pre-war talks from Warrenpoint, the paper also highlighted a letter sent to his anxious parents by a new recruit to the Royal Navy – 18-year-old Keith Scott from Kilkeel – who was sailing towards the Gulf on board HMS *Ark Royal*.

My own contribution to the Gulf War coverage was the telephone interview I conducted with Seaforde nurse Amanda Heenan while she was on a break at her flat in Dhahran, Saudi Arabia. There was nothing particularly remarkable in that – apart from the fact that the city, including the area where Amanda lived, was under constant Scud missile attack by the Iraqis and she could have thrown herself under the table for protection at any point during our conversation. By Amanda's own admission she had "never been so frightened" in her life.

Journalism at its finest was evident in the series of reports my colleague Gary Hewitt wrote in the aftermath of the Loughinisland pub shootings. To place what he achieved in some sort of context, when the Heights Bar atrocity occurred, on 18 June 1994, in addition to myself we had a reporting staff of just three – Gary, sports editor Raymond Stewart and newly-recruited trainee Judith Farrell.

Gary was at the scene of the mass murder within an hour, spending the rest of that Saturday night and part of Sunday in Loughinisland.

He undertook to write all the reports, in addition to covering the funerals. Meanwhile, Raymond took care of the sport and between us Judith and I looked after all the other news for that week's edition, which went to press on the Tuesday night – some 72 hours after the attack which had left six local men dead and many others injured.

Gary's stories took up the first eight pages of the paper, which we determined should carry no advertising to mark the gravity of the situation, and earned him the praise of local community leaders for the sensitive manner he had approached his work as a reporter, given the pain and anguish being experienced by so many people in the village.

Early in the New Year the *Mourne Observer* was in the running for a Newspaper of the Year award thanks to Gary's unstinting efforts the previous June. Events in Northern Ireland, however, had moved forward at an incredible pace in the intervening months, with the paramilitary ceasefires and their aftermath capturing all the headlines – and, as a result, all the awards that night at the Culloden Hotel.

In the end there was no mention of the *Mourne*

Dressed to the nines for the 1995 press awards in the Culloden Hotel. Back (from left): David Hawthorne, Terence Bowman, Gary Hewitt. Front: Chris Halpin and Judith Farrell.

Read All About It!

Observer and its Loughinisland coverage, nor any praise for the role played by Gary Hewitt and, it should be stressed, our photographers as well. To this day I will argue that the efforts of the *Mourne Observer*, and both the *Down Recorder* and the *Down Democrat*, going so far beyond anything they had ever been called upon to do in the past, merited recognition from their peers.

Several stories from the early years of the new Millennium stand head and shoulders above the rest, meriting specific mention. In terms of features (as opposed to news reporting), nothing surpasses Neil Loughran's evocative two-page reflection on the Mourne potato pickers of the 1960s.

Reporter Gary Hewitt chose to leave Radio Foyle in 1991 for the security of a full-time job with the *Mourne Observer*.

It had a very simple genesis, being born out of a press release issued by Ulster Television to promote a new series of archive programmes hosted by Julian Simmons. It included a still picture from a mid-1960s film showing two schoolchildren, a boy and a girl, in a field picking potatoes. In those days many country schools, especially in Mourne, were permitted to allow pupils to take time off from class to assist with vital farm work.

My first thought was to make a few discreet enquiries to determine if the children featured in the photograph were still living locally and, if so, would it be possible to get them together to recreate that scene for the *Mourne Observer*. Not only were Marie Trainor and Eamon

Cunningham still in the district, they were also very happy to comply. Neil instinctively felt there could be much more to the story and went along with the photographer to sound them out.

Sure enough, both had plenty of tales to tell about the era of the potato pickers and the resulting interview, published the following week, was a feature that easily matched any from the 1950s and 1960s when the *Mourne Observer*, still a relative newcomer to the local newspaper scene, was breaking new ground in terms of recording and preserving many aspects of local history. It would have been a source of immense pride to Jim Hawthorne that the paper, through Neil Loughran on this occasion, was maintaining that fine tradition.

In 2008 the *Mourne Observer* welcomed new senior reporter Lisa Ramsden to the editorial team as Neil's replacement. She joined a small and very select group of journalists who had also worked not only for *The Outlook* in Rathfriland but also the *Down Recorder*, where she had spent almost a decade honing her writing skills. It wasn't long before her wish for new professional challenges was being answered – in the most dramatic of fashions.

That August, Newcastle was hit by some of the worst flooding in living memory. Large parts of the town were cut off from the outside world and many people had to be rescued from their homes as water levels rose to unprecedented levels. Lisa, a dedicated member of the local Coastguard Service in her spare time, not only undertook her responsibilities in that regard but also, over the course of the next few days, compiled reports that at the time were amongst the finest I had ever read in my years as Editor.

I was on leave and out of the country in November (2008), when Lisa surpassed her work on the flooding disaster, following a terrible road accident between Rostrevor and Warrenpoint, which claimed the lives

Lisa Ramsden – Northern Ireland Weekly Newspaper Reporter of the Year in 2009

of four police officers – all from South Down and all very well known in the community. Lisa, who was personally acquainted with several of the victims, set her own emotions to one side as she, with the support of acting Editor (and my very able successor) Stephen Patton, worked around the clock to complete her reports on the tragedy.

In March 2009, at the Europa Hotel in Belfast, Lisa was named Weekly Newspaper Reporter of the Year at the Press and Broadcast Awards organised by the Chartered Institute of Public Relations. It was an award she had neither sought nor ever expected to win. On the night she was accompanied by friends from all departments at the *Mourne Observer* and, put simply, her richly-deserved accolade that night ranks amongst the proudest moments in my professional career.

To end on a somewhat lighter note, some of the newspaper's most memorable stories – among them some very convincing April Fools' Day spoofs – have been published in the consistently popular *Man About Town* column.

It first appeared in the *Mourne Observer* following the paper's launch in October 1949

Lisa Ramsden (front, third from left) with Mourne Observer colleagues after receiving the Northern Ireland Weekly Newspaper Reporter of the Year accolade at the Europa Hotel in March 2009. Back (from left): Nicky McKenna, Michael Flanagan, Stephen Bleue, Ian Morris, Chris Halpin, Terence Bowman, Sean McDowell. Front: Carole Hawthorne, Alice Bleue and Stephen Patton. Picture by David Hawthorne and there was always plenty of speculation about the anonymous author's identity. The late J. D. Morgan was finally acknowledged as the first *Man About Town* following his death in the 1960s; thus it would certainly be no lie to admit the baton changed hands at least once.

The finger of suspicion was pointed in my direction on a few occasions but I can categorically refute the accusation. In truth, all I ever did was pass on notes and observations for his attention and the fact *Man About Town* very obviously supported Manchester United during much of my time at the paper was a pure coincidence.

If pressed on the identity of JD's successor, my money would be on the late and still greatly missed Dick Hall. If ever a man had his finger on the pulse of everything that was happening in Newcastle and district it was Dick, who had topped the poll back in the 1960s to win a seat as an Independent on the old Urban Council.

Former Newcastle Urban Councillors were reunited in the early 1990s for a special 'looking back' feature in the Mourne Observer. Back (from left): Sarsfield O'Flinn, Joe Keenan, Dick Hall. Front: Archie Cairns and Mrs L. B. Purdy.

He would be a definite contender for *Man About Town* – his column benefiting from tip-offs aplenty from regular contributor Leonard Charles, with added wisdom from the late Peter Burns, of Kettering, Northants (via Annsborough, outside Castlewellan), the *Mourne Observer*'s most prolific letter writer of all time. There again, I could be mistaken...

People power in South Down

Like any local newspaper worth its salt the *Mourne Observer* from its earliest days never shied away from supporting local community campaigns so long as they weren't party political or showed favour to one religious persuasion over another.

Controversial Kinahalla

An artist's impression of the proposed Kinahalla Dam which is to be built between Hen Mountain and the slopes of Kinahalla (left). Cock Mountain towers over the new dam and the Spelga Dam is on the top left with Kinahalla Youth Hostel on the lower right.
See: Water officials put case for new dam, Page 7. Also Col. 9 this page.

ANOTHER
MOURNE OBSERVER
EXCLUSIVE

During my time at the paper there was strong backing for the fight against a new reservoir planned for the Mournes, rejection of proposals to close many primary and secondary schools across the district, endorsement for numerous locally-based campaigns, for example demanding the provision of footpaths, safety barriers and other measures aimed at saving lives, and, of course, it played a leading role in the decades-long battle to save the Downe Hospital in Downpatrick from closure.

The uproar in 1978 and 1979 that greeted the proposed dam at Kinnahalla was the first major manifestation of 'people power' that I witnessed. Having played a major role in breaking the story in the first place, the *Mourne Observer* then provided a vital platform for the many local protest groups that sprang up in opposition to the plan.

Certainly there were some who argued in favour of the many – albeit temporary – jobs the construction work would create and even the recreational use that could be made of a large expanse of water, but such support was decidedly thin on the ground.

The main anti-dam organisation was the Kingdom Of Mourne Residents Against the Destruction of the Environment (KOMRADE), led by the

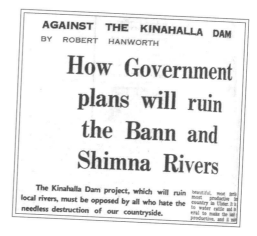

AGAINST THE KINAHALLA DAM
BY ROBERT HANWORTH

How Government plans will ruin the Bann and Shimna Rivers

The Kinahalla Dam project, which will ruin local rivers, must be opposed by all who hate the needless destruction of our countryside.

tireless Dr Arthur Mitchell, who almost single-handedly succeeded in placing the protection of the environment high on the political agenda at a time when the Troubles dominated the headlines.

Another important voice raised in the fight against the controversial project was that of *Mourne Observer* correspondent Robert Hanworth. Arguing in October 1978 that there was no justification whatsoever for the plan to build another dam, he said it would ruin many local rivers, including the Shimna and the Bann, and "must be opposed by all who hate the needless destruction of our local countryside."

Most readers would have been unaware that the author was, in fact, Will (William Robert) Hawthorne and the important role my late mentor played in corralling public opposition to the project cannot be overstated.

Kinnahalla became the subject of a public enquiry which opened in Newcastle in May 1979 with an inspector hearing opposing sides of the argument over a period of some months. He ultimately ruled against the plan, which had already cost the taxpayer around £775,000, and it was formally abandoned in 1980. There was a brief attempt to revive the scheme about a decade later but that too came to nothing. History shows the campaigners were absolutely right to take their stand against Kinnahalla as no demand was ever shown to exist for an additional water supply from the Mournes.

In more recent years the *Mourne Observer* chose not to favour one group over the other in the debate regarding a proposed National Park for the Mournes, largely because it became clear very quickly that reasoned arguments were being articulated by each side. While it was a decision that most likely did not win us too many friends among the more vociferous anti-Park campaigners, we preferred to make the newspaper's columns freely available to all with a point to make. In doing so we reasoned the general public would be better placed to make up their minds on the subject.

Endorsing a local campaign to save a primary or secondary school

from the axe rarely ended in success as the Education Boards already had their minds made up long before a closure 'proposal' ever went out to consultation. Even those schools initially given a reprieve were very quickly under threat again as the authorities just changed the criteria – usually based around the numbers attending a particular school.

Sticking to the 'numbers game' all too often meant only limited thought was given to the devastating impact a school closure would have on the community it served. Back in the late 1980s there was massive resistance to the plan to amalgamate Castlewellan High School, Killyleagh High School and Quoile High School (Downpatrick) into one single school in the County Town, later named Down Academy.

The main opposition centred on Castlewellan High School, which had first opened its doors in 1956 and during the course of the next 30 years catered for the educational needs of more than 2,100 students. Unusually for the time, Unionist and Nationalist politicians were completely united in emphasising the importance of retaining a state secondary school in an area with a sizeable Protestant community. Their pleas fell on deaf ears and the amalgamation went ahead in 1991.

The same fate awaited dozens of primary schools dotted around the

South Down countryside – all falling victim to the Education Board mantra that large was always better.

It was the *Mourne Observer* that pioneered the concept of 'First Schooldays' photographs back in the mid-1970s. While most newspapers at one time or another had photographed new arrivals at a few local schools, we visited every single one within our circulation area and indeed sometimes beyond it, gaining valuable additional sales. Very often there would be schools with just one or two new pupils and yet they were widely acclaimed as beacons of academic excellence.

As a camera-carrying reporter in my early days with the *Mourne Observer*, I had my own favourite schools when it came to mapping out the 'First Schooldays' routes. One in particular was the two-roomed Leitrim Primary School in the hilly countryside between Castlewellan and Ballyward. The story is told that it received a new computer from the Southern Education Board in the early 1980s but it remained stored in the box since the school didn't have a mains electricity supply but relied instead on an old-fashioned boiler, located in the centre of the main classroom, for heat and light in the winter months.

By 1987 Leitrim PS had 14 pupils under the care of Mrs Doris Kidd. The governors and parents argued that the school merited retention and modernisation as it served a specific rural community. Their plea, along with many others from around South Down, went unheeded; if anything there was a stepping-up of the closure programme during the remaining years of the 20th Century and, of course, similar 'hit lists' are still being drawn up and anti-closure campaigns are still being fought.

With the obvious exception of the Troubles, no other subject dominated the headlines more during the 1980s and 1990s than the unceasing campaign to save the Downe Hospital. Thankfully, it ultimately proved successful, although with the Department of Health forever moving the goalposts, ongoing vigilance to protect the services provided in the £64m complex is essential.

Back in March 1985 the *Mourne Observer* took the unprecedented step of launching a fighting fund with a £1,000 donation, while at the same

time announcing the formation of a new Area Support Group, initially consisting of Bill Martin, Rosaleen Torney, David Allister and Michael Boyd (Newcastle), Francis Gallagher (Castlewellan), plus Jim Cochrane and the Rev. C. D. Adams (Ballynahinch). The emphasis was very much on galvanising opposition in the three towns and surrounding districts, along with those parts of Mourne that looked to Downpatrick for their hospital services.

While it readily acknowledged that the main thrust had to come

from the County Town itself, where the hospitals and the local economy were under threat, the Area Support Group argued that people living in the outlying areas they represented would be the worst affected if the closures went ahead.

Among the first to lend the campaign their full support were Downpatrick's three SDLP Councillors, Eddie McGrady, Dermot Curran and John Ritchie, the latter stating: "We welcome the support and commitment of both our local papers and their great efforts to bring these issues before the public."

Over the following weeks and months membership of the Area

'Manning' the hospital campaign float (from left): Sean McDowell, Raphael Mason, Audrey Hodges, Seamus McConkey, David Hawthorne, Russell Bailie, Nicky McKenna, Nicky Cunningham. Front: Sean McConkey and Jim Perry

Support Group was boosted through the co-option of further members from villages and townlands in Down District and Mourne. The fundraising side of the campaign, carefully monitored by a group of trustees, was phenomenally successful and completely transparent. In each edition of the *Mourne Observer* we published the names of every person, business and organisation that had made a donation, large or small, during the previous seven days.

By the time it was agreed by the membership of the Area Support Group that the interests of the pro-hospitals campaign would be best served through a unified Down Community Health Committee, their Save Our Hospitals Fund had passed the £13,000 mark, approximately half the sum raised from the general public during the 1980s towards the defence of Downpatrick's hospital services.

No reflection on campaigning would be complete without a personal tribute to the indomitable Gerry Rice, the Drumaness father-of-11 who more than anyone epitomises my concept of the individual fighting on behalf of his family against 'The System' – in his case, Down District Council.

You can read his story,

Gerry and Gemma Rice

69

going back almost four decades, by typing 'Gerry Rice' and 'Smoke Nuisance' into any Internet search engine. In essence, back in 1976, not long after he and his wife Gemma moved into their new semi-detached home at Carlisle Park, Ballynahinch, Gerry noticed smoke in his front room which was clearly coming from his next door neighbour's fire.

It transpired that the houses had been built with honeycomb-like Terralux blocks, which by all accounts were not on the approved list of building materials for new houses in Northern Ireland. Gerry's campaign to reveal the presence of these blocks in many hundreds of homes throughout the county and the serious dangers they presented to the occupants, led to allegations of a massive cover-up.

Gerry stood for election to Westminster in 1979 as an Interdependence candidate, winning the support of 216 voters. He and Gemma contested the 1981 Council elections together, adding another 76 supporters to his cause. Ultimately Gerry's fight against 'The System' cost him his home, he had a criminal record (along with some 50 court appearances) and he was declared bankrupt – but not at the expense of his self-respect.

I pursued the story over many years for the *Mourne Observer*, affording Gerry space for the many letters he wrote and the statements he issued to keep the public abreast of his ongoing campaign. I also made a number of approaches to various Government agencies seeking 'their side of the story' with regard to the presence of Terralux blocks in thousands of County Down homes. Curiously enough, no one was every prepared to put down in writing that the homes were 100% risk-free.

One of Gerry's most high-profile supporters over the years has been the BAFTA award-winning television writer Jimmy McGovern (*Cracker, The Lakes, Hillsborough*). Jimmy penned an eloquent summary of Gerry's battles against authority and, in particular, Down District Council. What a riveting story he told... and what a television series it would make!

Tollymore area residents gathered together in 1995 to campaign for a proper footpath along the (still) dangerous Tollymore Road. Included in the picture are the late Cllr Gerry Douglas and the late Norman Jenkinson, retired news editor at the Belfast Telegraph and occasional stand-in Editor at the Mourne Observer.

Enjoying the 1985 summer festival parade in Newcastle (from left): Sally Bingham, Audrey Hodges, Sean McConkey, Maureen Hodges and Charlotte Hodges

Hughie and Colm

No account of life at the *Mourne Observer* would be complete without reference to Hughie Carville and Colm Murray. While management managed, reporters reported, typists typed and workers worked, nothing would ever have happened without the often combined endeavours of Hughie and Colm.

A wave to the camera from Hughie Carville in the late 1970s, with Colm Murray (left) included

Hughie was our van man for more than a decade, joining the paper in April 1976 after compulsory retirement at 65 had confronted him the previous month. During a long working life he'd held a number of driving positions, his previous employers having included the Ulster Transport Authority, the Forestry Service, Newcastle Urban Council and Down District Council.

Once recruited by the *Mourne Observer*, Hughie spent much of his day back on the road, gathering news, photographs and advertising from pick-up points the length and breadth of the county. No journey was too long for him (or, indeed, too short as he once accidentally steered a new van through the front office window!).

His collections around the district completed, Hughie would then join the late night production team, helping to parcel up the printed piles of *Mourne Observers* for delivery to a network comprising more than 120 newsagents. No prizes for guessing who took a lead role in that particular aspect of the operation.

Renowned for his brusque sense of humour and the obvious enjoyment he derived from the occasional modest wager ('two bob' was usually sufficient), there was barely a soul Hughie didn't know. He once told a reporter how he'd given her snowbound mother, then a young nurse, a lift back to Newcastle from Saintfield during the bad winter of 1963; she checked and of course it was true.

Sadly, Hughie is no longer with us. However, he went to his grave knowing the long-awaited scheme to replace all the old cottages at Wild Forest Lane, where he lived with his wife Rose, had been completed by the Housing

A last cup of tea for Hughie Carville in January 1987, pictured here with Nicky McKenna

Executive. He'd fought long and hard for those new houses and he was delighted when the work was done.

Colm Murray joined the *Mourne Observer* in 1973 and his job, literally, was to keep the wheels and cogs of the printing presses turning. He had arrived not long before the move from 47 Main Street to the new offices at Castlewellan Road.

As a skilled mechanic he played a pivotal role in the installation and ongoing maintenance of the new printing press and then again at the turn of the Eighties when the components for a second press were transported from assorted locations in Scotland and the Irish Republic for reassembly in Newcastle.

Ensuring both huge presses always ran smoothly, along with the other printing machines and assorted vehicles, was a full-time occupation.

However, Colm was very much a team player and he managed to set aside sufficient time for recreational activities organised by his colleagues outside (and occasionally inside) working hours.

A special publication to mark Colm Murray's retirement in November 2000

Colm at work on the final edition of the Church of Ireland Gazette to be printed by the Mourne Observer in Newcastle

He was the life and soul of any *Mourne Observer* gathering, but especially at Christmas – that time of year when staff members, young and old, finally had a chance to let down their hair at the annual party and almost risked calling The Boss by his first name. At the end of the night Colm would always be called upon to sing *White Christmas* and his word perfect rendition was guaranteed to bring a tear to the eye.

With the retirement of Hughie Carville at the beginning of 1987 and, two years later, the ending of newspaper printing in Newcastle, so too Colm's role within the company evolved. As well as keeping an eye on the various machines the company had retained for other printing purposes, Colm took on the dual role of collecting the adverts and other material, as well as delivering the papers.

Unlike Hughie, however, Colm very deliberately brought his 27-year career at the *Mourne Observer* to a close at the end of November 2000. Retirement was something he'd looked forward to and today both he and wife Bernie remain very familiar figures around the town. Indeed, there are one or two places where Colm is particularly familiar!

Mourne Observer Memories

While the feat of the four Hawthorne sisters (Lottie, Mary, Maureen and Evelyn), who all worked for the paper at one time or another, will surely never be equalled, two sets of sisters have worked for the Mourne Observer – Annabell Ogle and Isabell Hamilton, and Judith Farrell and Paula Newell. Indeed, Paula's daughter Vicki also worked for the company.

Twenty-five year veterans – Colm Murray and Raymond Stewart with David Hawthorne (centre) in September 1998

Management and staff gathered at the Donard Hotel in January 1987 to bid a fond farewell to Hughie Carville, who was retiring for a second time - having joined the staff at the age of 65 in 1976. Back (from left): David Hawthorne, Lottie Hodges, Alice Bleue, Sally Bingham, Anne McConnell (later Tremlett), Valerie Keown, Maureen McClean, Kathleen Braniff, Edna Prytherch, Evelyn Connor, Regina O'Hare, Mary Erwin, Maureen Hodges (later Harrison), Anne-Marie McAleenan, Clifford Mills, Nigel Croskery, Colm Murray, Irene McGrady, Isabell Hamilton, Jim Hawthorne. Front: Kathleen O'Hagan, Stephen Bleue, Richard Truesdale, Sean McDowell, Raymond Stewart, Terence Bowman, Jimmy Mills, Hughie Carville, David Telford, Ken Purdy, Nicky McKenna, Eugene Bannon, Raphael Mason, Sean McConkey and Nicky Cunningham.

A proud and lasting legacy

The final years of the 1980s witnessed the appointment of two noteworthy additions to the busy editorial and photographic departments.

As we approached the seismic changeover to a very different production system and a new-look *Mourne Observer* in April 1989,

The editorial team in April 1989, when the smaller format Mourne Observer was introduced. From left: Terence Bowman, Amy Biggerstaff (later Dempster), David Telford and Raymond Stewart.

reporter Paul McCreary indicated his intention to move on to a new job, leaving us in urgent need of a replacement to work alongside Raymond Stewart, David Telford and myself.

Some 18 months earlier The Boss had recruited teenager Amy Biggerstaff to the small army of keyboard operators who spent several hectic days each week working their way through a veritable mountain of edited copy – typed and handwritten – for inclusion in the paper. She had impressive credentials, having just completed the Private Secretaries Certificate course at Downpatrick College, which included shorthand and typewriting skills. Nor did it do any harm that she was a granddaughter of the late David Biggerstaff, who had served as our West Down correspondent for many years.

In addition to her role in the *Mourne Observer* 'typing pool', Amy would occasionally contribute short news items and concert reviews, the quality of which impressed me considerably. At the time I was still attending Newry and Mourne Council and Newry Magistrates' Court, and so, very often during her own free time, she would accompany me for the experience of seeing what a journalist's work entailed.

Over a period of some months Amy built up a sizeable portfolio of published material; it was little wonder then that The Boss endorsed my recommendation that she should be invited to join the editorial team as Paul's replacement.

It seemed the perfect solution but it also created a very real problem for Amy. While the prospect of becoming a full-time newspaper reporter was certainly exciting, she was also concerned that if it didn't work out she might end up with no job at all, as the paper would need to replace her in the setting room.

Thankfully, Amy decided to give it a go – we shared an office as well as coffee-making and plant-watering duties – and thus began a wholly unplanned writing career that continues to the present day. Over the following months her general reporting duties included courts and assorted public meetings, but her true forte very quickly emerged – as a feature writer with an innate ability to very quickly win the trust of the person she was interviewing.

'A day in the life of our coastal rescue services' – a feature by Amy Biggerstaff from June 1989

Stories on subjects as diverse as flying a helicopter, the route taken by water from the Silent Valley reservoir to the tap, the Mourne Mountain Rescue Team, Neil Powell's mountain rescue dogs and the work of the Newcastle RNLI crew (which included being airlifted out of the lifeboat in the middle of Dundrum Bay), all added to the ever-improving content of the *Mourne Observer*.

Marriage to husband David in 1990 and the subsequent arrival of daughters Rachel and Stephanie ultimately saw Amy bringing her career at the paper to a close in 2002. However, during 2013 she dusted down her shorthand notebook and conducted a series of interviews for *The Ards in the Sixties*, the latest publication from Ballyhay Books of Donaghadee.

The second addition in the run-up to the changeover was Chris Halpin, the youngest new recruit for a decade. We were approached in October 1988 about the possibility of taking him on under the employer-based Youth Training Programme run by Hugh J. O'Boyle Ltd. in Downpatrick. Chris had helped with a story published in the

New recruit Chris Halpin, recipient of a Youth Training Programme award in March 1988, with Terence Bowman at the awards evening in Downpatrick

Mourne Observer the previous year when he was still at school in Ballynahinch. The enthusiasm he showed then was enough to gain him a trainee placement and, within six months, a full-time staff job.

Initially Chris had set his sights on becoming a reporter and several stories carrying his by-line appeared in the paper. However, as with Amy and feature writing, his keen eye for a picture emerged very quickly and he joined the photographic team which then consisted of Eugene Bannon and David Longlands.

Chris Halpin, now working with long-serving stalwarts Pat O'Hare and Michael Flanagan, is the paper's longest-serving photographer and one of the élite corps of staff members to pass the quarter-century mark.

That Jim Hawthorne should have played a prominent role in the recruitment of both teenagers indicated his continuing involvement in the day-to-day running of the *Mourne Observer* and also his desire to see the paper moving forward with a new generation to work alongside the 'old hands'.

In similar vein, over a period of several years The Boss had been handing over managerial responsibilities to son David who, to all intents and purposes was running the business by the early 1990s.

However, there was still one more major writing assignment for Jim Hawthorne, who turned 80 in 1993 and whose career in newspapers stretched back in 1929. Over the years the *Mourne Observer* had gained itself a formidable reputation as the publisher of numerous local history books, the main

The largest selling paper in the history of the Mourne Observer was the edition published on 18 September 1991 – three days after Down's Gaelic football team had secured the fourth of five All Ireland titles. We printed an unprecedented 17,000 papers that week and sold them all.

aim being to preserve such valuable material for posterity. Examples included the reprinting of W. G. Lyttle's acclaimed 19th Century novel *Betsy Gray* in 1968 (with further editions in future years) and *The Dam Builders*, Harold Carson's unique tribute to the men who built the Silent Valley Reservoir (1981).

In addition, the paper carried many articles relating to our past by, amongst others, Fiona Jones (née Doyle), Bill McStay, John Bryce, J. S. Doran and Horace Reid.

That was the motivation behind his decision to publish a revised edition of *Sailing Ships of Mourne*. First released back in the early 1970s and containing splendid chapters by Will Hawthorne and Ken Purdy, as well as Annalong writer W. J. Fitzpatrick, it was highly regarded among seafarers and historians alike. However, always the perfectionist, The Boss had long harboured suspicions about the accuracy of other aspects to the book. In truth, only he would have noticed.

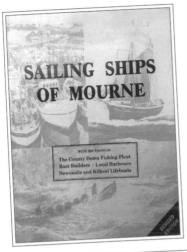

Jim Hawthorne went on to devote much of his time over the next two years to revising the original chapters and adding material to *Sailing Ships of Mourne*. There was certainly no question of him sitting behind a desk staring at a computer screen to do this; rather, The Boss spent many days out and about interviewing anyone and everyone associated with the fishing and boatbuilding industries.

In doing so he turned an already good book into a great one – dedicated to Will and the late W. J. Fitzpatrick – that sits alongside the *Mourne Observer* as a proud and lasting legacy to his skills as a writer and editor. Regrettably, while The Boss was one of the first people to hold a copy of his new *Sailing Ships of Mourne*, by then he had already suffered the debilitating stroke that would eventually bring about his death.

After a career in newspapers that spanned almost 66 years he passed away, aged 82, on 22 March 1996. Responsibility for drawing together the many tributes fell on my shoulders. It was not a duty I took lightly and hopefully, a little older and a little wiser, I managed to do his memory justice.

All the same, no one succeeded in capturing the very essence of our founder more than his old adversary Colin Crichton, owner of the *Down Recorder*:

A man of Jim Hawthorne's extensive ability is not likely to be found again in our lifetime. Firstly, industrial circumstances do not allow it; secondly, such was his mastery of all aspects of his work that he could have produced his newspaper single-handedly if time were of no importance.

One of life's remarkable men whose mind never halted, he will be remembered for his half century's realism in newspaper's history. A firm, indeed an institution in himself, he was a stirringly energetic creator, driver and disciplinarian with a quest for perfection in all he did or was done for him.

His work was his pleasure and, largely, his reason for living. Unmatched in effort, he liked being first in and last out of the building, even seven days a week if necessary, having a finger in every pie and an eye ahead.

Full of ingenuity, canny, cute and inventive, he relished his capacity to fill many men's shoes and outplay most of them. With his passing comes reflection. By today's standards, his life's work was exemplary in terms of meeting his obligation to all around him and to the public he served.

If he measured life's worth by personal output, he was in a dynamic league of his own. He could use courage and defiance as readily as charm or compassion, yet his unpretentious, unassuming personality remained as solid as his sincerity of purpose.

Positively direct, if need be, he was intolerant of sham. His riveting perseverance inspired the finding of better ways and other outlets for his painstaking flair and timeless skills.

For all his dynamism and strong opinions, he enjoyed listening. Diplomacy and tact were ready attributes, as were his sympathetic ear or willing hand, open, welcome and uncomplicated.

More than most, his life was lived fully and usefully to the greater good of individuals and organisations encountered on the way. His name will come up in conversations for generations to come. To have known him and worked with him represented an education not otherwise generally available.

Read All About It!

Jim Hawthorne in September 1993, around the time he commenced work on the revised edition of Sailing Ships of Mourne. Picture by James Aiken.

Our golden jubilee in October 1999 was marked by BBC Northern Ireland, which dedicated an entire edition of *Country Times* to a week in the life of the *Mourne Observer*. Presented by Donna Traynor with additional reporting by Kim Lenaghan, the programme featured most members of staff but the star 'turns' were undoubtedly Alan McVeigh and Meloney Imrie, as well as Nicky McKenna and Raymond Stewart.

Charlotte Hawthorne, an influential figure in her own right during the formative years of the paper and beyond, posed proudly with son David, daughter-in-law Carole and the entire staff for a photograph to mark the *Mourne Observer*'s first 50 years. It appears on the front cover of this book. A celebration dinner followed in the Slieve Donard Hotel; memories of The Boss were rarely far from anyone's lips.

David and Carole Hawthorne with David's mother Charlotte, widow of Mourne Observer founder Jim Hawthorne, in October 1999, marking the paper's 50th anniversary. Mrs Hawthorne, who passed away in April 2010, was predeceased by son Will (February 1984) and daughter Evelyn (May 2003).

Mourne Observer Memories from 1976-2011

Farewell gifts were presented to Evelyn Connor following her retirement in March 1993. Back (from left): Terence Bowman, Raphael Mason, Jim Myall, Anne McConnell (Tremlett from the following May), Jim Aiken, Alice Bleue, Nicky McKenna, May Magee, Kathleen Braniff, Adelaide Richie, Gary Hewitt, Valerie Keown, Kathleen Ward, Irene McGrady, Sean McDowell, Isabell Hamilton, Sean McConkey, Chris Halpin. Front: Amy Dempster, Colm Murray, Jim Hawthorne, Evelyn Connor, Basil Connor, David Hawthorne and Carole Hawthorne.

Nicky McKenna (third from left) receives a gift in 1995 to mark his 25 years' service with the Mourne Observer. From left: Stephen Bleue, Jim Aiken and David Hawthorne.

Raymond Stewart and Colm Murray (seated) jointly celebrated 25 years at the Mourne Observer in September 1998. New additions to the staff at that time included Paula Newell (back, seventh from left) and Margaret Polin (front, centre).

The editorial team in October 1999 (from left): Amy Dempster, Raymond Stewart, Meloney Imrie, Terence Bowman and Alan McVeigh.

83

Environment Minister Peter Bottomley (right) visited the Mourne Observer in June 1990. Here he is shown one of the final pages made while production of the newspaper was still in Newcastle. From left: Terence Bowman, Jim Hawthorne and David Hawthorne.

Completing a hat trick of Ministerial visits (after Brian Mawhinney and Peter Bottomley), Jeremy Hanley, who carried both the Health and Agriculture portfolios in the early 1990s, helps to put together one of the sports pages. From left: David Hawthorne, Raymond Stewart and Jim Hawthorne.

Worn out after working exceptionally late one Tuesday night in the early 1990s to complete the sports pages in Raymond Stewart's absence are (from left): Terence Bowman, Sean McConkey, Raphael Mason and Stephen Bleue. The clock shows 12.45am but, in truth, it had been moved forward about two hours for the photograph!

Celebrating a rare hot summer's day in 1995 (from left): Adrian Hanna, Stephen Bleue, Raphael Mason, Sean McDowell and Nicky McKenna

Farewell presentations to Adrian Hanna in August 1996. From left: Christobel Sanderson, Isabell Hamilton, Esther Malcomson, Sharon Paulson, Raymond Stewart, Terence Bowman, Alan McVeigh, Adrian Hanna, Pat O'Hare, Grace Hanna (Martin from the following month), Sean McDowell, Maureen McClean, Tonya Rogan, Deirdre Rooney, Nicky McKenna, Lindsay Fergus, Stephen Bleue and Alice Bleue.

A mid-1990s message for photographer Pat O'Hare that his beloved Aston Villa were under-performing (again). From left: Sean McDowell, Stephen Bleue, Chris Halpin, Raphael Mason and Colm Murray.

Looks like Stephen Bleue (left) won a wager with Pat O'Hare

85

Read All About It!

Bidding farewell to Tonya Rogan (front) in 1997 on the occasion of her marriage. From left: Sharon Paulson, Valerie Keown, Alan McVeigh, Raymond Stewart, Alice Bleue, Sean McDowell, Lindsay Fergus, Terence Bowman, Stephen Bleue, Annie Cooper, Nicky McKenna, Jim Aiken, Niki Hill, Esther Malcomson, Grace Martin, Raphael Mason, Michael Flanagan, Eileen Mitten and Deirdre Rooney.

Celebrating a 'significant' birthday for proof reader Niki Hill (holding balloon with reference to year in question). Back (from left): Grace Martin, Eileen Mitten, Isabell Hamilton, Christobel Sanderson, Paula Newell, Deirdre Rooney, Alice Bleue. Front: Margaret Polin, Sharon Paulson, Esther Malcomson and Valerie Keown.

Pictured at a lunch in the Burrendale Hotel to mark Raymond Stewart's 25 years' service are (back, from left): Raphael Mason, Chris Halpin, Michael Flanagan, Terence Bowman, Amy Dempster, John McCance, Meloney Imrie, Nicky McKenna, Gary Hewitt. Front: Ken Purdy, David Hawthorne, Sean McDowell, Raymond Stewart, Alan McVeigh, Lindsay Fergus and David Telford.

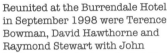

Reunited at the Burrendale Hotel in September 1998 were Terence Bowman, David Hawthorne and Raymond Stewart with John McCance, who had worked at the Mourne Observer for about 10 years in the 1970s and 1980s. John was also a renowned wedding photographer, who covered the marriages of many staff members over the years. He died in September 2000 and is fondly remembered by his family circle and Mourne Observer colleagues.

Bidding farewell to Jim Aiken (fourth from left) in October 1999 after a career with the Mourne Observer that had spanned some 12 years. From left: David Hawthorne, Terence Bowman, Raphael Mason, Stephen Bleue, Valerie Keown, Sean McDowell, Grace Martin, Raymond Stewart, Nicky McKenna, Alice Bleue, Deirdre Rooney, Margaret Polin, Christina Murnion (later Doran), Jayne Galway (later Gill) and Meloney Imrie. Sadly, Jim passed away in July 2006. He is greatly missed by his family and many friends.

Farewell to Lindsay Fergus (front) in the autumn of 1997. Back (from left): Valerie Keown, Chris Halpin, Colm Murray, Alice Bleue, Anne Tremlett, Nicky McKenna, Terence Bowman, Stephen Bleue, Michael Flanagan, Meloney Imrie, Karen Law, Deirdre Rooney, Sharon Paulson. Front: Sean McDowell, Raymond Stewart, Grace Martin and Christobel Sanderson.

87

Read All About It!

Stephen Bleue (left) and Nicky McKenna work with one of the Heidelberg machines that remained operational long after printing of the Mourne Observer ceased in Newcastle

Senior members of the production staff in October 1999. From left: Nicky McKenna, Jim Aiken, Raphael Mason, Sean McDowell and Stephen Bleue.

The sports pages

The Newcastle summer festival programme of 1982 offered local people and holidaymakers a charity fundraiser with a difference – a football challenge match between the inappropriately named *Mourne Observer* All Stars and the *Down Recorder* Dynamos.

Although we were fierce rivals when it came to our work, there was nevertheless a healthy, albeit unspoken, respect between the staffs of the two newspapers. This was largely because of an acceptance that if **we** were putting in ridiculously long hours each week to produce the *Mourne Observer*, then most likely so too were they as far as the *Recorder* was concerned.

Quite who first came up with the idea of the Donard Park encounter, which took place on Saturday 31 July, has long been lost in the mists of time but the amazing

Mourne Observer Memories

Irwyn McKibbin was goalkeeper for three Irish League clubs – Cliftonville, Derry City and Linfield between the late 1960s and mid-1970s. He was also on the Irish Amateur International side which won the British Championships. These days he is perhaps best known for his work with the Heartbeat NI charity.

Irwyn McKibbin is captured by the author in goalkeeping action for Derry City against Bangor in the early 1970s. The Bangor player is Mourne man Jim Graham.

Read All About It!

fact is that the game, which was well promoted during the festival, actually attracted a sizeable crowd (certainly more than the proverbial man and his dog that most of us had expected).

We had hoped to coax Council chairman Cecil Maxwell along to hand over the equally inappropriately named 'Sweet FA Cup' to the winning team but at the last minute his services were required elsewhere and that happy duty fell to our owner, Jim Hawthorne. Well, it would have been happy on the basis that our *Recorder* opponents won the first half and we then won the second, suggesting the match had finished an honourable draw. Regrettably, however, the four goals they hammered past us before the break made all the difference. The final score was 5-2 in their favour and The Boss somehow still managed a broad smile as he presented the trophy to *Recorder* captain Joe McCoubrey.

The Mourne Observer All-Stars soccer team in July 1982. Back (from left): Will Hawthorne, Johnston Lewis, Sean McConkey, Harry McKibbin, Stephen Bleue, Raymond Stewart, John McCance. Front: Duncan Ramsden, David McCavery, Terence Bowman, Eugene Bannon, Paddy Killen and David Craig.

The victorious Down Recorder Dynamos. Back (from left): Paul Synott, Adrian Carson, John Moore, Gary Law, Paul Symington, Harry McCurry. Front: Charlie Oakes, Chris Hagan, Joe McCoubrey, Johnny McCoubrey, Marcus Crichton and Seamus McGivern.

Of course, the real winners that day were the good people who ran

90

the Ruby House holiday home for handicapped children in Newcastle. A collection among the public and the players, generously supported after the final whistle by Jim Hawthorne and his *Recorder* counterpart Colin Crichton, raised in excess of £130 for a particularly fine local cause.

Down Recorder captain Joe McCoubrey accepts the trophy from Jim Hawthorne.

For the record, the home side's scorers were Paddy Killen and Raymond Stewart (who are both still working for the paper, the former as an accomplished freelance photographer and the latter as its long-serving and highly respected sports editor), while the *Recorder* had Chris Hagan (2), Joe McCoubrey and Seamus McGivern (2) to thank for their… I write this with gritted teeth… well-deserved victory.

After conceding it might be better to drop the All Stars bit from our name, we agreed the *Mourne Observer* soccer team

VICTORY . . . AT LAST

The Mourne Observer's football team, readers will be pleased to learn, has recorded its first victory after three unsuccessful outings. The win came last Friday night and for once I can actually record the final score, 4-1 to the lads. Their thanks go out to the opposition, a team comprising members of Newcastle's Malaysian student population with a few local players to complete the numbers.

There's no truth to the rumour that the Mourne Observer squad is seeking a return fixture in the Malaysian students' home country!

actually had a future, not least as an extra-curricular way of maintaining the very obvious spirit of camaraderie that existed within the workplace. Matches followed in quick succession against Newry and Mourne Council staff in Kilkeel and the *Tyrone Courier* in Dungannon, with both ending in heavy defeats for us. Undeterred, our first victory, with an amazing 4-1 scoreline, was recorded early in September over a team comprising members of Newcastle's surprisingly large Malaysian student population.

Perhaps we should have called it a day at that point but we decided to soldier on, taking on teachers from St Malachy's High School in Castlewellan, assorted Boy Scouts and the might of the RUC in Newcastle (watched over from a distance by heavily-armed colleagues) – all in preparation, as we saw it, for the long-anticipated revenge fixture with the *Down Recorder*. The challenge, when it came from our friends in Downpatrick, was that rather than another outdoor encounter, we might care to 'do battle' in a number of different disciplines at the Down Leisure Centre in Downpatrick.

We accepted without hesitation. Reasoning that the Newcastle Festival result was just an aberration – all down to the colour of our shirts – we reckoned we would have them over a proverbial barrel given our team members' individual sporting accomplishments. However, much to Irish international Stephen Bleue's disappointment, the list of sports did not include indoor bowls. Nor was there a road race along the streets of Downpatrick which would have suited Raphael Mason and Nicky Cunningham – acclaimed in our office, if nowhere else, for a gruelling challenge run over a three-mile Newcastle circuit one quiet afternoon when The Boss was away (Raphael won after Nicky opted for a speedy start and then very quickly ran out of steam).

The Mourne Observer soccer team in 1983. Back (from left): David Telford, Hugh Robinson, Sean McConkey, Brian Hodges, Raphael Mason, Eugene Bannon, John McCance. Front: Jim Perry, Terence Bowman, David McCavery, Nicky Cunningham, David Craig and Russell Bailie.

History thus records that the 'oul enemy' won every single event, the sole exception being something called the 'unihoc element'. Thankfully, Jim Hawthorne wasn't around that evening to witness our shame-faced retreat from Downpatrick.

Over the following years, and despite increasing responsibilities all round at the *Mourne Observer*, we somehow maintained our sporting interests – although there might be an argument over whether a few hands of cards at lunchtime actually constituted 'sport'. For some of us, though, there were highly energetic Wednesday morning table tennis sessions in the Newcastle Centre after the paper was delivered to the shops. By that stage, in the latter part of the 1980s, the *Mourne Observer* was being printed at our Newcastle offices throughout the night, and there was really no better way any of us could think of for blowing away the cobwebs after a virtually non-stop 18-hour working day.

There was never any room for religion or politics within the workplace banter at the Mourne Observer, but football – that was a different matter! This is a list of the English soccer teams supported by different staff members down the years:

Arsenal – Eugene Bannon, Michael Flanagan, Alan McVeigh, Meloney Imrie

Aston Villa – Pat O'Hare

Bolton Wanderers – Irwyn McKibbin

Everton – Sean McDowell

Leeds United – Stephen Bleue, Colm Murray, Raymond Stewart

Liverpool – Chris Halpin, Gary Hewitt, Stephen Patton, Ken Purdy

Manchester United – Terence Bowman, Gavin Gallagher, Emmett Gilmore, Aaron Hawthorne, Valerie Keown, Gavin Lonergan, Neil Loughran, John McCance, David Telford

Newcastle United – Niall Burns

West Ham United – Raphael Mason

There was a brief attempt to revive the football team around that time. A further heavy loss, this time to the *County Down Spectator* in Bangor, coupled with some particularly scathing remarks the following week from their renowned columnist Colin Bateman, failed to deter us.

However, our footballing exploits in the Eighties (the decade – not our ages) did finally come to an end following a highly embarrassing defeat at the hands of a newly-formed team whose pitch was little more than a muddy field in a staunchly loyalist part of West Down. There was a half-serious suggestion before the kick-off that to protect our Catholic players from any risk of unintentional harm we should shout 'Willie' when trying to attract a player's attention. It didn't matter in the end – our opponents treated us with the greatest respect but still thumped us 14-1. 'Willie' scored our goal.

The combined Mourne Observer and Down Recorder cricket teams from around 1990. At the front, Dundrum Cricket Club's Jeff Maguire with respective captains David Telford and Andy Campbell. Back includes: Stephen Bleue, Chris Halpin, Raphael Mason, Paul Symington, Gordon Symington, David Campbell. Front: Johnny McCoubrey, Terence Bowman, Eugene Bannon, Marcus Crichton, Raymond Stewart, Gary Law and Michael Flanagan. Picture by Bill Hamilton.

The best part of the day was the hour or three we spent afterwards with our new friends in the Ulster Arms. After that, with the exception of a soccer match against a *Down Democrat* XI in the mid-1990s, the under-performing *Mourne Observer* football team called it a day.

However, that wasn't quite the end of the sporting story. Over the years there were two cricketing encounters between the *Mourne Observer* and the *Down Recorder* and hosted by Dundrum Cricket Club. The first was so long ago, around 1990, that David Telford was our captain – and yet, despite having that advantage, the margin of the *Recorder's* victory was considerable.

As for the second encounter, that one took place on Friday 30 August 1996, a day that will forever be remembered and celebrated by... the *Mourne Observer*! Yes, we finally beat the hoodoo, brought down that proverbial Berlin Wall between Downpatrick and Newcastle and saw off our bogey team – Andy Campbell and all – with a display that brought back memories of the fondly remembered day at Sion Mills in 1969 when Ireland bowled out the West Indies for just 25 runs. The victory came in a tense 20-over match and our roll of honour included batting heroes Chris Halpin and the aforementioned Stephen Bleue, with the winning run coming from Paddy Killen. Did we gloat in the pub afterwards? Too right we did!

As for me, I tore a muscle in my back thanks to my fielding endeavours and, being a matter of months away from my 40th birthday, got a less than subtle warning from my doctor that it was perhaps time to turn my attention to more sedate outdoor activities, like gardening. Mrs Bowman concurred.

That's more like it! The victorious Mourne Observer cricket stars lord it over the vanquished Down Recorder team in the final (so far) sporting encounter between the two newspapers. Included are: Gary Law, Paul Symington, Marcus Crichton, Charlie McStay and Andy Campbell (for the Down Recorder), and Alan McVeigh, Terence Bowman, Chris Halpin, Michael Flanagan, Paddy Killen and Stephen Bleue (Mourne Observer).

New Millennium, new challenges

We welcomed the year 2000 with one of the most strikingly symbolic front page photographs in the *Mourne Observer*'s history, which by then stretched back more than 50 years. Pat O'Hare's ethereal image of the Legananny Dolmen at dawn, captured in the most vivid colours, perfectly combined one of the district's best preserved pre-Christian artefacts with the community's prayerful hopes for continued better times ahead.

Terence Bowman was next to join the Twenty-Five Year Club in June 2001, with colleagues old and new attending a lunch at the Enniskeen Hotel. Latest recruit to the editorial team was Neil Loughran (standing, left).

Maybe it was just an age thing (mine!), but as far our editorial team was concerned, and this is not intended in any way to be disrespectful to those who brought their not inconsiderable talents to the *Mourne Observer*, the door now seemed to be revolving considerably more quickly than it ever had in the past. While arrivals and departures in the first 15 years of my career at the paper could have been counted, literally, on the fingers of one hand, by the beginning of the new Millennium the whole concept of taking on a raw teenager and turning him or her into a fully–fledged journalist after an in-house training period of maybe three or four years was very much a thing of the past.

Instead, if a member of the team decided to move on after a few years, their replacement would almost always be someone with similar experience from another local newspaper. Such a policy – and it was certainly not confined to the *Mourne Observer* – offered only limited prospects to the large numbers enrolling on official training courses. Indeed at one point Meloney Imrie at 27 was our youngest reporter, which was certainly a far cry from 1976 when Raymond Stewart and I were still teenagers with considerable responsibilities on our young shoulders.

As a result I found it was becoming increasing difficult to form the sort of bond with a new team member that in the past would have been the makings of a lifelong friendship.

Coupled with a swiftly changing editorial team was the unrelenting infiltration of email into our working lives. There had been more

The editorial team at the beginning of 2002 (back, from left): Raymond Stewart, Neil Loughran, Alan McVeigh, Terence Bowman. Front: Amy Dempster and Meloney Imrie. Meloney and Alan, who left the Mourne Observer in 2002 and 2003 respectively, were married in August 2005 and now have a daughter, Erin.

than a hint of what was to come with the installation of a fax machine in the mid-1990s. In earlier times local politicians had personally delivered their typed or handwritten statements to the office or else had dictated a few sentences over the telephone to a reporter with the required shorthand skills. One or two of the savvier ones realised their statements could be circulated to two or three newspapers thanks to a couple of sheets of well-worn carbon paper but in general there was a decidedly personal touch to their contacts with the paper.

Thanks to the fax machine and its seemingly endless rolls of paper we witnessed the first hints of mass news distribution at the touch of a button.

However, it was the advent of email that very quickly saw the art of issuing political statements being raised to an entirely different level. Not only could our publicity-minded representatives send the same email message to a half-dozen local papers, they could also seek the attention of the dailies, along with assorted local radio and television stations. All too often a very mundane statement about a hazardous pothole along a local country lane would feature

Bidding farewell to Grace Martin in 2004. New recruits included Niall Burns, Gavin Lonergan and Jason Hill.

on a quiet day in the Belfast press long before the *Mourne Observer* appeared in the shops.

Not unsurprisingly, we even had a few politicians taking umbrage at the fact we'd highlighted only a couple of their statements despite the fact they'd issued a dozen or more during the course of the week. They were the same ones who, in earlier times, would have carried a tape measure to ensure they were getting the same column inches as their political opponents.

Another source of irritation to me – and some might suggest that is putting it mildly – was the emergence of the party political 'Letter to the Editor'. Back in the mid-1980s a group of pub-based Newcastle wags, clearly with too much spare time on their hands, had set themselves the challenge of getting a ridiculously inane anonymous letter published in the paper. Word filtered through about their intentions and I spent the next few weeks going through each letter with the proverbial fine toothcomb to ensure their ruse didn't succeed.

However, it was in the post-Good Friday Agreement era that the politically-motivated letters really started to flow. Most of the main political parties of that time indulged in the practice, which went along the lines of "I'm a disillusioned ex-DUP/Sinn Fein/SDLP/Ulster

Unionist voter and I want to express my anger at the way they've let down supporters..." It didn't take a genius to work out the letters were being conjured up by rival party spin doctors to wind up opponents, particularly in the run-up to anything that was remotely contentious.

The letters became increasingly bitter, very often carrying unsubstantiated and potentially libellous allegations about named individuals, and all, of course, requesting anonymity. While such letters were often accompanied by genuine names and addresses, they were being sent under false pretences – the culprits reasoning we wouldn't bother to check them since the identification information wasn't going to be published anyway.

The *Mourne Observer* finally called a halt to this unsavoury practice, taking a stand that others in the industry gradually began to follow. In future, we told readers, all letters of a party political nature would include, in print, the contributor's full name and address. A daytime contact telephone number was also required and I had no hesitation in confirming the bona fides of each and every letter writer prior to publication.

Needless to say, the political parties soon worked out a way to get around our efforts to take some of the heat out of the angry exchanges that featured all too often in the letters column. Sympathisers agreed to allow their names and addresses to accompany lengthy political essays penned by a paid press officer back at party HQ. Evidence of this could be seen in the fact that very often the same letters appeared in newspapers around the country, the sole difference being the name and address of the contributor. I never ceased to marvel at those previously silent men and women in our local communities who overnight became experts in many issues of local, national and international importance!

More than ever before I also found myself on high alert for anything at all that could give rise to legal action being taken against the *Mourne Observer*. Part of the special buzz I'd always experienced from seeing a brand new paper on sale in the shops each Wednesday was being spoiled by a nagging awareness that people were poring over every page in the hope of finding something they could take to a solicitor and then demand compensation.

Certainly long gone were the days when a quick telephone call could iron out any legal hiccups. On one memorable occasion in the early 1990s we accidentally transposed two photographs, resulting in a newly appointed bank manager winning a pub darts tournament and vice versa. The following day I received a solicitor's letter, not on behalf of the aggrieved bank manager but, amazingly, the darts player who claimed he was being ridiculed by his neighbours.

I rang the solicitor, a man I knew very well from my years attending the local courts, and expressed incredulity that such a strong-arm approach was deemed necessary. He replied: "For goodness' sake don't take it seriously – I'm getting paid legal aid money for writing the letter and that's an end to the matter as far as I'm concerned." He was as good as his word.

The truth is that our reporters always took the greatest care with their work, something that was drummed into them from the very beginning. Of course, mistakes did arise from time to time but there was never any malicious intent on our part and errors were corrected as appropriate. It was thanks to that cautious approach, coupled with careful scrutiny and the expertise of our own legal representatives, that at no point in all my years at the *Mourne Observer* were we ever successfully sued over anything we had published.

September 2008 marked the departure of long-serving proof reader Niki Hill (seated, second from left) for a new life in France. Back (from left): Paddy Quinn, Chris Halpin, Donna Cowan (later O'Flaherty), Niall Burns, Emmett Gilmore, Vicki Newell, Pat O'Hare, Ian Morris, Michael Flanagan. Front: Lisa Ramsden, Liz McCamley and Julie McLaughlin.

All the same, the enjoyment I'd always derived from the job started to wane and I began to wonder – having entered my 50s and discovered the years didn't stop rushing by – whether I really wanted to keep doing it for much longer. Coming from someone who had frequently asked the office staff to post me a copy of the *Mourne Observer* to my holiday address abroad, that was quite an admission.

Earlier in my career I'd been involved in putting together two books in my spare time – one was a compilation of features that had appeared in the *Mourne Observer* in 1991 (*Railway Memories*) and the other, in 1997, a more time-consuming biography of my great grandfather Alexander Bowman (*People's Champion*). Both had given me immense personal and professional satisfaction and, thanks to an encouraging public response, I came to the conclusion I had more to offer in that particular regard.

Following an approach by Newcastle Chamber of Commerce in 2005, I agreed to research and write *Places That Time Forgot*, a slim volume identifying places of special historical significance around the town. Three years later I followed it up with a specially commissioned centenary history of the *First Newcastle Scout Troop*.

Realising that much of my writing career had involved

The 30 August 2006 edition of the Mourne Observer marked the introduction of the compact tabloid format that exists to the present day. Production moved on that date from Portadown to Interpress, based at Duncrue Street.

By that time pages no longer needed to be delivered to the printers in negative form; rather, they were sent by broadband (which had been preceded by an ISDN line, the initials standing for Integrated Services Digital Network).

Many of Northern Ireland's weekly newspapers are now printed on the same presses, including the Down Recorder.

stories about other people, I commenced work in 2009 on a new personal project that had lain dormant in the back of my mind for many years. The concept was simple enough – a childhood memoir under the title *Bangor Boy*, recalling an assortment of experiences from my early years in the town. Of course, it didn't take me too long to realise that such a publication, whatever form it took, would have a decidedly limited appeal. The answer lay in expanding the content to include the memories of some 35 other men and women and, thanks to the generous support of the *County Down Spectator*, a large selection of photographs that few would have seen since the week they were published.

Long-serving proof reader Irene McGrady's daughter Niamh, who spent her school work experience with the Mourne Observer, appeared on Broadway in the Chichester Festival Theatre production of Macbeth in April and May 2008. The play, staged at the Lyceum Theatre, starred Patrick Stewart (of Star Trek: The Next Generation fame). Filmed for television, it was subsequently screened on BBC4. More recently, Niamh has had a recurring part in Holby City (BBC1) and a key role as a young policewoman in the BBC2 drama The Fall, which was set in Belfast.

The result was *Bangor in the Sixties,* put together with the help of former *Mourne Observer* colleagues Jason Hill (layout and design) and Niki Hill (proof reading), and published by Ballyhay Books of Donaghadee. The book attracted considerable favourable publicity and in Irish terms was deemed a bestseller. What I'd found particularly appealing during the research stage was that it offered me a chance to get out and meet people, something I'd largely – by choice – left to colleagues for the best part of two decades at the *Mourne Observer*.

It was a feeling I liked very much, but I also realised the time had come to make the big decision – more books or stay at the *Mourne Observer*. There weren't enough hours in the day for both and, having discussed the matter at length with my wife, the books option came out on top. Averil was very much aware my father had died when he was just 49 and that I had no great desire to put things off till I was 65, or older, and then hope I'd still be healthy enough to fulfil an assortment of ambitions.

I told David Hawthorne in July 2010 and promised I wouldn't be going anywhere for another six months. My only request was that he and his wife Carole wouldn't try to talk me out of it – and he was as good as his word. It was also taken as read that Stephen Patton would become Editor with Lisa Ramsden as his deputy. Along with Raymond Stewart, they were advised of my plans before the summer was out, with the rest of the staff hearing the news before the end of November. To say they were surprised would be an understatement; I had been a permanent fixture at the paper for nearly 35 years – literally, as during all that time I had missed work due to illness on only one occasion and that was back in 1979.

My final paper was the Christmas 2010 edition, although I kept a close eye on the incoming news and feature material until New Year's Eve when Averil and I set off for a short break in England. I pulled the office door behind me one last time and that was that. Officially I remained on the company books into the first week in January, which meant I'd been employed by the *Mourne Observer* between 1976 and 2011. I was, at that time, the fourth longest continuously employed member of staff in the paper's history after Nicky McKenna, Raymond Stewart and Sean McDowell, but I was very happy to know I would be losing my place in that particular ongoing challenge.

To refer back to Raymond one last time, during all the years we worked together at the *Mourne Observer*, sharing a considerable amount of time in each other's company, we never exchanged as much as a sharp word or argued about anything, except perhaps football. Given the constant pressures around us, that was quite an achievement.

A few Christmases ago we went out for lunch together, just the two of us having a mutual grumble about working such long hours. It was something, we agreed, that hadn't changed since we were teenagers. Unlike the bill that day – which was considerably more than the pound we'd each paid for a three-course lunch back in the 1970s!

Within weeks of leaving the paper I'd commenced work on a sequel, *Bangor in the Seventies*, to be followed a year later by *Bangor in the Eighties*. And now, as I write these closing lines, a fourth volume is set for release, covering *The Ards in the Sixties*.

Never, for even a millisecond, have I regretted the decision to bring my time at the *Mourne Observer* to an end. I don't miss the unrelenting demands the job placed on my time and my life. I do, of course, miss the day-to-day contact with friends at work, especially those who shared my journey over so many years. We laughed together and we cried together; we attended each other's weddings and family celebrations, and when death robbed us of a loved one, we were there for each other.

Footnote: My time with the *Mourne Observer* added up to 12,602 days, equivalent to 1,800 weeks (and editions of the paper) or 302,448 hours. Not that I was counting!

Colleagues past and present, as well as Down Recorder Editor Paul Symington (extreme right) attended the author's farewell dinner at the Buck's Head Inn, Dundrum, in March 2011. New staff members included Heather Stevenson, Emma Wallace, Laura Hawthorne, Claire McLaughlin and Kathryn Gracey. Front row: Carole Hawthorne, Ken Purdy, Terence and Averil Bowman, Dominic Cunningham and David Hawthorne.

A trio of new members to the Twenty-Five Year Club in July 2002, namely Isabell Hamilton, Stephen Bleue and Irene McGrady (at front). New staff member Gavin Gallagher is included. Picture by James Aiken

Stephen Bleue shocks Raphael Mason by taking an unscheduled break

Meloney Imrie moved on to pastures new in early 2002 after spending more than four years as a valued member of the editorial team.

Jaki Wilson (seated, centre) moved to London in 2003 after a short stint in the editorial department.

Read All About It!

Long-serving reporter Alan McVeigh left the Mourne Observer in the autumn of 2003. New staff member Anne Dornan (to the left of Deirdre Rooney) is included.

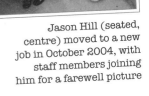

Jason Hill (seated, centre) moved to a new job in October 2004, with staff members joining him for a farewell picture

The Enniskeen Hotel was the venue in the summer of 2004, when Alice Bleue joined the Twenty-Five Year Club. Back (from left): Irene McGrady, Niki Hill, Isabell Hamilton, Christina Doran, Margaret Polin, Jayne Galway (later Gill), Marie Burton, Eileen Mitten, Valerie Keown, Meloney Imrie, Sharon Paulson, Esther Malcomson. Middle: Raymond Stewart, Paula Newell, Deirdre Rooney, Gavin Lonergan, Stephen Patton, Colm Murray, Alan McVeigh, Neil Loughran, Grace Martin, Anne Tremlett, Jason Hill. Front: Carole Hawthorne, David Hawthorne, Stephen and Alice Bleue, Terence Bowman and Nicky McKenna.

The Mourne Observer family

Freda Adair
James Aiken
Lydia Annett
Ryan Armstrong
Russell Bailie
Eugene Bannon
Mark Barr
Marie Bartley
Jean Bell
Amy Biggerstaff/ Dempster
Sally Bingham
Sue Bishopp
Stephen and Alice (née Kerr)
Bleue
Jean Bolton
Terence Bowman
Kathleen Braniff
Ellen Brennan
Anne Brown
Charlie Brown
Marbeth Brown
Moya Burns
Niall Burns
Marie Burton
Ann Carr
Hugh Carville
Freda Cave

Janet Chambers
Kellie Chambers
Len Churms
Bridie Clendenning
Albert Colmer
Paddy Comiskey
Evelyn Connor
Annie Cooper
Julie Cooper/ McLaughlin
Eleanor Cope
Jackie Coulter
Donna Cowan/ O'Flaherty
David Craig
Andrew Cromie
Kenny Cromie
Nigel Croskery
Bronagh Cunningham
Celine Cunningham
Marion Cunningham
Nicky Cunningham
John Dick (Sen.)
Anne Dornan
Frances Dunseith
Gail Edgar
Valerie Edgar/ Keown
Diane Erwin
Mary Erwin (née Hawthorne)

Read All About It!

Madge Ewart
Judith Farrell
Barbara Fegan
Lindsay Fergus
Michael Flanagan
Diane Forbes
Eileen Forsythe
Evelyn Forsythe (née Hawthorne)
Paul Fullam
Brendan Gallagher
Gavin Gallagher
Jayne Galway/ Gill
Zita Gibson
Emmett Gilmore
Kathryn Gracey
Gerry Grant
Noel Halliday
Chris Halpin
Isabell Hamilton
Adrian Hanna
Grace Hanna/ Martin
James Hanna
Lillian Hanna
Jim Harrison
Nell Hawkins
Aaron Hawthorne
David and Carole Hawthorne
Jim and Charlotte Hawthorne
Laura Hawthorne
Will and Mary Hawthorne
Anthony Heaney
Olive Hempsey
Lee Henry
Gary Hewitt

Gary Hill
Jason Hill
Niki Hill
Brian Hodges
Hugh Hodges
Lottie Hodges (née Hawthorne)
Maureen Hodges/ Harrison
Meloney Imrie
Norman Jenkinson
David Kennedy
Paddy Killen
Gary Law
Karen Law
Peter Lawson
Johnston Lewis
Rose Lewis
Gavin Lonergan
David Longlands
Neil Loughran
Anne Lyle
Anne-Marie McAleenan
Phil McArdle
Liz McCamley
Marlene McCammon
John McCance
Dessie McCartan
David McCavery
Maureen McClean (née Hawthorne)
Michael McClean
Elizabeth McCleery
Jackie McConkey
Seamus McConkey
Sean McConkey
Anne McConnell/ Tremlett

Paul McCreary
Sean McDowell
Elizabeth McGivern
Irene McGrady
Louise McHenry
Nicky McKenna
Peter McKibben
Irwyn McKibbin
Claire McLaughlin
Jim McMurray
Doreen McNeilly
Edna McNeilly
Gwenda McNeilly
Mike McNulty
Alan McVeigh
May Magee
Mrs Magill
David Mahood
Esther Malcomson
Raphael Mason
Phyllis Mateer
Martin Mawhinney
Sam Maxwell
Jean Miller
Clifford Mills
Jimmy Mills
Peter Mills
Eileen Mitten
Hugo Moore
Bernadette Morgan
Mollie Morgan
Ian Morris
Christina Murnion/ Doran
Bridie Murphy
Colm Murray

Jim Myall
Paula Newell
Vicki Newell
Annabell Ogle
Kathleen O'Hagan
Anne O'Hare
Pat O'Hare
Regina O'Hare
Dessie O'Neill
Ann O'Reilly
Noreen Parks
Stephen Patton
Sharon Paulson
Jim Perry
Margaret Polin
Harry Polland
Roberta Priestley
Edna Prytherch
Jo Purdy
Ken Purdy
Douglas Quail
Paddy Quinn
Duncan Ramsden
Lisa Ramsden
Alice Redfern
Adelaide Richie
Pam Riley
Hugh Robinson
Fiona Rodgers
Tonya Rogan
Deirdre Rooney
Philomena Rooney
Laurence Rowe
Margaret Rusk
Christobel Sanderson

Read All About It!

Elizabeth Sloan	Richard Truesdale
Paul Smyth	Anne-Marie Wallace
Eileen Spence-Hammond	Emma Wallace
Heather Stevenson	Kathleen Ward
Raymond Stewart	Jaki Wilson
David Telford	Ryan Woodside

Every effort has been made to ensure the accuracy of this list, which aims to include all those associated with the *Mourne Observer* from circa 1975 to the present day. While most are/were members of staff, the list also includes short-term reporters, freelance photographers and contributors who, in the main, worked only for the *Mourne Observer* and regularly visited our offices in Newcastle.

The cut-off point was those who worked at Castlewellan Road, following the move there from 47 Main Street. Since the list relies largely on memory and photographs, there is every possibility that some names will have been omitted, for which an apology is extended in advance. Female employees are identified by the name they were known by when working at the paper, with their married name being included only where the person in question married while working for the paper.

In addition to Will Hawthorne, three staff members died in service during the period in question – compositor David Kennedy (as the result of a road accident), senior typesetter Harry Polland and proof reader Adelaide Richie. All are remembered by their work colleagues.

Please contact the author by email, terence.bowman@btinternet. com, with any corrections or additions to the list. Should there be a reprint of the book, efforts will be made to update the list of names and any other errors that come to light.